W9-AFO-109

Australia's Last Explorer:
Ernest Giles

Great Travellers

General Editor: George Woodcock

Bokhara Burnes
James Lunt

Henry Walter Bates, Naturalist of the Amazons
George Woodcock

Thomas Gage in Spanish America
Norman Newton

Alexander Mackenzie and the North West
Roy Daniells

some other books by Geoffrey Dutton

Founder of a City: The Life of William Light
(*F. W. Cheshire, Melbourne, and Chapman and Hall, London*)

The Hero as Murderer: The Life of Edward John Eyre
(*Wm. Collins, London, and F. W. Cheshire, Melbourne*)

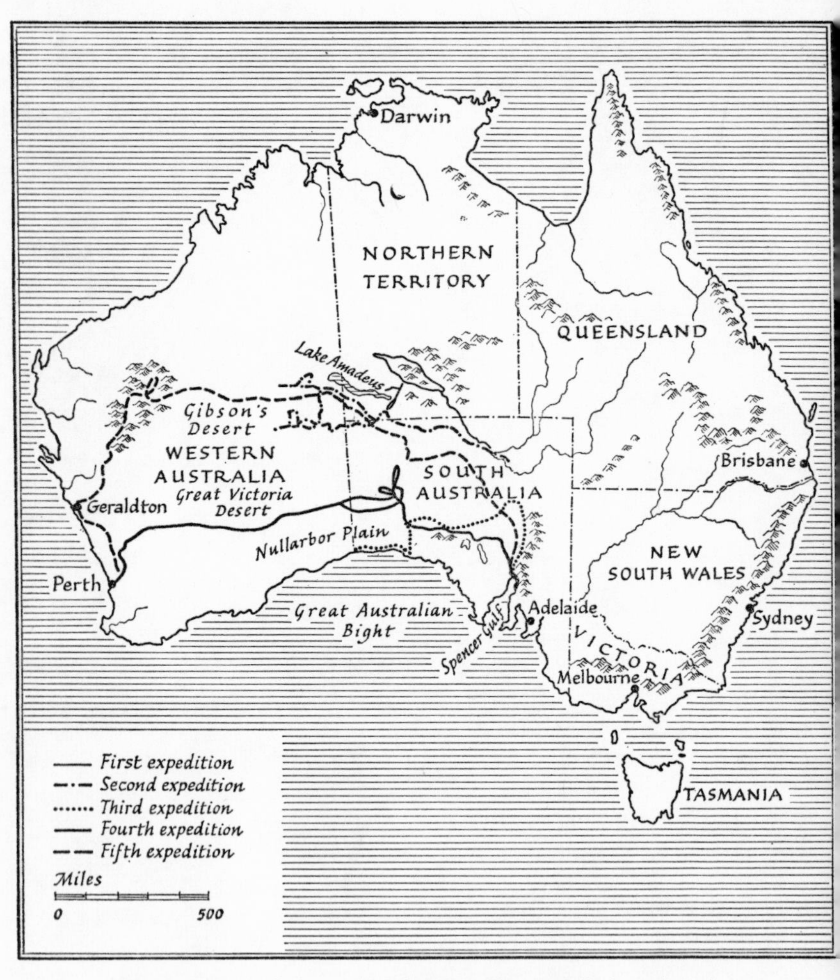

General map of Australia showing Ernest Giles' explorations

AUSTRALIA'S LAST EXPLORER: ERNEST GILES

by

Geoffrey Dutton

BARNES & NOBLE, Inc.
NEW YORK
PUBLISHERS & BOOKSELLERS SINCE 1873

First published in 1970
by Faber and Faber Limited

First published in the United States, 1970
by Barnes & Noble, Inc.

SBN 389 03974 8

Printed in Great Britain

For

Randolph Stow

Acknowledgements

My grateful thanks for assistance in research are due to Mr. Hedley Brideson, Mr. Gerald Fischer and the staff of the South Australian Archives and the State Library of South Australia; Miss Paula Nagel; Mr. Neville Green; Mrs. Dorothy Moore, and Miss Vicky Gordon.

Thanks are due to Mr. Len Beadell, and to the publishers, Rigby Ltd., for permission to quote from *Too Long In The Bush*, by Len Beadell.

NOTE

Most of the direct quotations from Giles himself are taken from *Australia Twice Traversed* (1889). Occasionally a fuller version is given from one or other of his two earlier books listed in the Select Bibliography on page 170.

Contents

Illustrations

PLATES

MAPS

I

The Unexplored West

Of all the great unexplored regions of the world, none subjected explorers to more consistent humiliation than Central and Western Australia. An area the size of the whole of Western Europe lured these fly-tormented men on from waterhole to watersoak with promises of an inland sea, of great rivers, of plains where millions of sheep and cattle could run, but in most cases nothing more was achieved than a connection between existing settlements. Unlike North America, Australia was settled around its edges, a nibbling, heartless approach to living that has persisted to the present day. Most modern Australians have never been inland except as tourists, insulated from the shocks of dust and distance. The myth of the outback is the heart of the country's identity, while the citydwellers look outwards to the sea. There is no Chicago, Kansas City or Dallas in the middle of Australia, only a small town called Alice Springs, and five hundred miles in any direction much the same emptiness that engulfed the first explorers. West of Alice Springs, despite all the excitements of mineral discoveries, there is still a thousand miles of red emptiness.

The crossing of the continent from south to north connected Australia to the rest of the world with a stronger link than any in a ship's anchor chain. One of the most important moments in Australian history came on 21 October 1872 when the Overland Telegraph began operation, and for the first time, in Charles Todd's words, 'the Australian Colonies were connected with the grand electric chain which unites all the nations of the earth'.

For those still wanting to investigate the huge unexplored areas of Australia, the Overland Telegraph was a lifeline. Until 1872 almost all Australian exploration had radiated from centres of settlement. Eyre stumbled from Adelaide to Perth, Burke and Wills set out from Melbourne to the Gulf of Carpentaria in hopes of returning to Melbourne, Sturt left from Adelaide with a boat to launch on an inland sea. But in the 1870's Giles, Gosse, Warburton and Forrest all made journeys which began or ended at the centre, under the wires of the Overland Telegraph. The final welcome in Adelaide or Perth, the champagne, the feasting and the Mayor's platitudes, were irrelevant noises off, compared with the silence of the interior crossed only by the hum of the telegraph wire.

S. T. Coleridge wrote of 'that willing suspension of disbelief for the moment, which constitutes poetic faith'; the fierce poetry of Central and Western Australia demanded such a faith from its explorers, as well as courage and endurance. For Eyre, Giles and Warburton in particular, there were many moments in which the only certain thing should have been a disbelief in survival. But they went on, and survived, often only by luck. Moreover, in a broader sense, they refused to disbelieve in the country itself. The mallee scrub, the red parallels of the sandhills, the clay or salt pans like smooth, healed burns on the earth's skin, the needles of the spinifex drawing blood from the horses or camels, not to mention the heat and the flies, should have made them cynically reject the country. But they accepted its impossibilities, even if some of them fired guns into the natives whose existence proved that survival was possible. And none of them knew anything of the gold, iron or nickel their boots were crossing.

The most poetical of all the explorers was Ernest Giles, although the intensity of Eyre's experience made him the one from whom most poetry could be made. But Giles adored poetry, and carried volumes of it around in his mind instantly available for response to every fresh, amazing sight. The names he gave these harsh realities are a wild Golden Treasury: The Vale of Tempe, Zoe's Glen, the Fairies' Glen, Titania's Spring, the Ruined Ramparts, Dante's Inferno. There are chapter headings in his narrative like 'Extract from Byron for breakfast'. Like Byron, he cheerfully admitted the sublime and the absurd, and often laughed that he might not weep. There are quotations from the poets scattered like auriferous stones across the country of his narrative, and sometimes there are odd outcrops of what appear to be his own verses. When he discovered something 'truly wonderful' like Mount Olga his response is poetic, not scientific, his imagination leaps for comparisons: 'it is composed of several enormous rounded stoneshapes, like the backs of several monstrous kneeling pink elephants.'

He populates this land devoid of written history with memories of European civilization, revealing again the poetic mind that admits the happy coexistence of imagination and actuality. Giles saw nothing bizarre in sitting on a sand-hill in the wastes of South Australia 'having one of those extraordinary waking dreams which occasionally descend upon imaginative mortals', when 'the imagination can revel only in the marvellous, the mysterious, and the mythical'. Yet, unlike Eyre and Grey, although capable of human sympathy with the Australian aborigine he is quite incapable of responding to what is 'marvellous, mysterious and mythical' in their beliefs. When 'Mr. Murray's black boy' tells them of the monstrous serpent that crawled 400 miles from the Musgrave Ranges to Fowler's Bay, he laughs at 'the absurdity of his notions', and says the story of the serpent and its subsequent adventures 'would have made an excellent novel, which might be produced under the title of "Black Romance"'.

Giles has a Chaucerian love of created things, animals, men, nature, with that sense of comedy that extends to his own inadequacies or failures. He is the only one of the explorers who is not afraid to admit the absurdities of many of the humiliations inflicted on them by the country. In this he also has the true bushman's sense of humour, which is based on his own incongruity in face of the malignity of inanimate things, the stubbornness of animals and the crankiness of human beings. While proud of the grandeurs and agonies of his experiences, Giles is always modestly, humorously conscious of being a small bony man with a high, domed forehead and a straggly moustache, wearing an overcoat of flies, fighting his way thousands of miles to discover little but desert. No explorers had harder journeys, or discovered less of apparent value, than those who crossed the West of Australia. They were amazingly philosophic about it, but none more so than Giles, who after reaching Perth in 1875 wrote to Sir Thomas Elder: 'I travelled during the expedition 2,500 miles, and unfortunately no areas of country available for settlement were found. The explorer does not make the country, he must take it as he finds it; and though to the discoverer of the finest regions the greatest applause is awarded, yet it should be borne in mind that the difficulties of travelling such a country cannot be nearly so great as those which confront the less fortunate traveller who finds himself surrounded by heartless deserts. Still, the successful penetration of such a region has its value, both in a commercial and scientific sense, as it points out to the future emigrant or settler those portions of our continent which he should most religiously shun.'

What is truly astounding is, that having written such a letter, and helped drink all the champagne in Perth, Giles should have turned round and taken his camels all the way back again, travelling by a route 400 miles north of his East-West track, deliberately making for Gibson's Desert which had nearly killed him, and in which Gibson had perished, in 1874. One is reminded of Eyre on his journey around the Great Australian Bight, who, having chanced at his last extremity on Captain Rossiter's whaler, calmly went back on shore again and finished his journey to King George's Sound.

For such men there was no reward expected, and precious little given. In an age such as the present, when all motives seem smirched by commercialism or dogma, these explorers have the purity of the rocks and birds they moved amongst. As Giles wrote at the end of his narrative, 'An explorer is an explorer from love, and it is nature, not art that makes him so.'

However, it takes more than a leader to make an expedition, however much he may love exploring, and it is notable that Giles' right-hand man, W. H. Tietkens, who lived till 1933, always spoke of his old leader with affection and admiration, and that Alec Ross, who was on the third expedition, wrote in 1928, 'Giles was a man of undaunted courage, and a born leader.'

II

Early Days

William Ernest Powell Giles was born in Bristol, England on 20 July 1835, the eldest son of William and Jane Elizabeth Giles. He went to school in London at Christ's Hospital in Newgate Street, famous as the Blue Coat school from its dress of a blue gown, with knee-breeches, a yellow petticoat and stockings, neckbands and blue cap. One can scarcely imagine a more incongruous background for an Australian explorer, but in fact it is fairly typical; almost all of them were born in Great Britain, Europe or India, the sons of minor gentry, army officers or parsons, and educated accordingly. Native sons like W. C. Wentworth or John Forrest were very much the exception. It is one of the miracles of history that a few years after leaving some English school these men were leading expeditions through the unknown outback of Australia.

Ernest Giles must have studied hard at Christ's Hospital, for he had the essentials of a good classical and literary education by the time he was fifteen, when he emigrated to Australia. His parents, his brother and his five sisters had gone a year before, in 1849, and he joined them in Adelaide. It was a bad time to come to South Australia. In 1851 the population was 63,700, but in that year gold was discovered at Ballarat and Bendigo and other places in Victoria, and within a few months more than a third of the adult males had crossed the border, taking with them two-thirds of the colony's coin. While South Australia was nearly collapsing, young Ernest followed the rush, but he had no luck on the goldfields, and fell back on a humdrum job as a clerk in the Melbourne General Post Office. There was a slight variation in situation, if not in excitement, when he became clerk of a county court.

In his early twenties he left the city, and took various jobs on stations along the upper River Darling, an area still very lightly settled, with scarcely explored country to the north and west. It was at Menindee, on the River Darling, that Burke and Wills established a depot on their journey to the Gulf of Carpentaria. Early in 1861 Giles was investigating new country north of Menindee for a station owner, with an assistant named Conn (later 'not only killed but partly eaten by the wild natives of Australia' near Cooktown on the Queensland coast). They spent some time in the area, turning back only eighty miles from Cooper's Creek, as Conn refused to go any further out. Had Giles kept going, he might have found Burke and Wills and King, who had just achieved the most famous near miss in Australian history; having crossed the continent, they tottered in to the Cooper's Creek Depot on 21 April 1861 just seven hours after the departure of Brahe and the rest of the party, who had awaited their arrival for more than four months. Later in the year Giles met Howitt and his expedition coming north in search of Burke and Wills; in September 1861 Howitt rescued King, the only survivor of the expedition.

This rather aimless life up and down the Darling, and over the ocean-like horizon of the almost unknown plains on each side of the brown river hidden by its escort of trees, made Giles into an expert bushman, something never achieved by some explorers, and only learned the hard way by others in the course of their expeditions.

Late in 1864 Giles was down in Melbourne again, and when visiting an old Post Office friend called Fagan, he met a young man of twenty, William Henry Tietkens, also an old Blue Coat boy from Christ's Hospital. It was the start of a long friendship, cemented by thousands of miles of dust and heat. Tietkens was a stocky man, even shorter than Giles, with a firm chin beneath a moustache and side-whiskers, with humorous eyes and a tolerant expression. He needed it, having already experienced enough hard times to fill a Victorian novel.

He was born in London on 30 August 1844, and his father, a solicitor, died when he was very young. He was sent to the Blue Coat school, but when he was fifteen his mother decided he should go to Australia. He went out alone to Adelaide, where he was to be under the care of an actor, G. A. T. Woods, an old friend of his mother's. He handed over his money to his guardian, who promptly went to the nearest pub and finished the evening, young Tietkens' first in Australia, locked up for drunken and disorderly conduct and assaulting the police.

Harry Tietkens was given a room in Woods' lodgings at the rear of the Theatre Royal, where it was announced that 'Mr. George Woods, the Eminent Tragedian' was engaged for a short season. Harry got a job as errand boy for everyone behind the scenes in the theatre. He stuck it out for six months when the Eminent Tragedian disappeared, leaving, in Tietkens' words, 'me and his landlady lamenting'.

Solomon, the lessee of the theatre, gave Harry another job as barman and bottle washer in his pub, and then a letter came from the shameless George Woods, asking Harry to join him in Geelong, Victoria, and please to bring the clothes he had left behind when he fled. Solomon paid Tietkens' passage on a paddle steamer, but he was broke when he left Adelaide, and had to take a job with a waggoner going to the Victorian gold diggings. At Castlemaine he met 'Uncle' George who took what free cash he had and told him to go to hell.

Tietkens compromised by taking various jobs such as newsboy, and cattleminder at Chinaman's Creek. 'What, it will be asked,' wrote Tietkens in 1920, 'could be the attraction for a boy of some culture in following so indolent a life, so inferior a position? It is hard to explain now, but the freedom from my uncle's restraint, the fact of making money, for it *was* money in my eyes at that age, everything gave me pleasure. The fresh bright morning air, the birds and flowers, the morning gallop on the barebacked pony, were all new and wonderful sources of pleasure.'

Later he made his way to Melbourne where he worked for a while as gardener to a Catholic bookseller, where he was required to jolly up the baby by pushing him around in a wheelbarrow. In later life he remembered being given his lunch one day wrapped in two pages of Byron's *Hebrew Melodies*; he begged for the rest and learned them by heart. He lost the job with the bookseller by tipping the baby into a puddle one day, and became a greengrocer's boy.

Unfortunately Uncle George now appeared again and was all charm and solicitude until he disappeared with Harry's savings for a year, and his father's watch. A Mrs. Hubbard, the landlady of a boarding house, took pity on Harry, and managed to get him a job selling tickets at St. Kilda railway station, at £50 a year. He kept this for three years, guarded perhaps too solicitously by Mrs. Hubbard, who was 'a woman of impulse and passionate to a degree'.

Now in 1864, Ernest Giles, this man from the bush, was there in the boarding house telling him about the vast Australia Tietkens had never seen, waiting to be explored by adventurous souls. Moreover, Giles was a Blue Coat boy. Giles urged Tietkens to come with him up the Darling. 'He recounted a few of his Bush experiences and fixed me with a desire for a life that seemed to me full of romance and adventure.' But Mrs. Hubbard was not losing her darling boarder; 'she would not hear of my giving up a position in which she said I was sure to advance.' Just then an opportunity for promotion in the railways came up, and Tietkens was passed over for some stranger with 'influence'. Somehow young Harry found the courage to tell Mrs. Hubbard he was going up the bush with Giles.

Giles was travelling to the Upper Darling, taking five or six horses, and striking out into the interior to report for a Melbourne firm on the country west of the river. He and Tietkens left at daybreak on New Year's Day 1865. 'That night,' wrote Tietkens later in his 'Reminiscences', 'we camped near Sunbury. It was my first night of really camping out, of lying on the ground with nothing over my blankets but a canopy of foliage, and well I remember the first strange impressions. The strange new voices of the night, the plaintive note of the curlew, the occasional shriek of the night hawk, the occasional remonstrance of a disturbed magpie, the jingling of our horse bells and the hoarse mutterings of opossums; all filled me with strange feelings that for some little time kept me awake.' For both of the young men the bush life was freedom, freedom from the General Post Office, the St. Kilda railway station, and Mrs. Hubbard. 'Everything was new and beautiful to me and I thoroughly enjoyed it. In the evenings over the camp fire we used to talk about the old school, or Giles would relate some of his experiences since he left there.'

They crossed the River Murray at Swan Hill in a canoe borrowed from the blacks, and then had to cross the Murrumbidgee which was seven miles wide in flood. After that there was no water, except at isolated settlements, for a couple of hundred miles until they reached Mt. Murchison on the Darling (now called Wilcannia). A hundred and fifty miles further on they rested at the outermost station, and then struck out north-west into almost unknown country, steering by compass. At Torowoto Swamp they crossed the tracks of Burke's party, still plainly visible, and then went on across fine saltbush country, the claypans holding sheets of water from recent rains, until they reached another famous explorer's depot, Charles Sturt's Depot Glen where the party took refuge in 1845 for six months during the hottest time of the year (later the settlement of Milparinka grew up nearby). They found fragments of Sturt's boat, brought to sail on that elusive inland sea so many explorers searched for, and the initials, carved on a grevillea tree, of poor James Poole, Sturt's second-in-command who died at Depot Glen. They also found a chain thrown over a mulga tree; at the top the wood had grown over the chain. For two more or less novice Australian explorers, could more haunting symbols of their profession be found? The rotting boat, that never found water on which to float; the dead man's initials on the tree; the hard mulga wood making a new link across the chain.

They stayed several days enjoying 'the Sylvan beauties' of Depot Glen, as Tietkens described them, with plenty of feed and water for the horses, and then struck north-east for Tongowoko Swamp near the Queensland border, where Burke and Wills had made a camp, leaving a lot of broken crockery behind them. They then headed back over rich pastoral country to Mt. Murchison.

Here Giles' commission was completed, and he made south for Melbourne, while Tietkens joined a party taking a mob of fat cattle down to Adelaide. The journey with Giles had made

Tietkens into a bushman, and when 'after three months of excessive hardship' he reached Adelaide he found he no longer cared for city life. 'I suppose I felt myself unsuited for town life for I had no trade or profession that would secure me a living in the busy haunts of men, or whether it was the keen remembrance of genteel and dependent poverty endured in Melbourne with Mrs. Hubbard I cannot remember. . . .' So for the next few years he wandered through the bush, taking various jobs, the most permanent of which was that of storekeeper at Corona Station, where the manager was a friend of Giles. Giles did not lose track of him, and in 1873 sent him a telegram asking Tietkens to join him on his Second Expedition.

Meanwhile this intermittent semi-exploring did not satisfy Giles, whose eyes had long been on the West, where a man could be 'the first to penetrate into this unknown region, where, for a thousand miles in a straight line, no white man's foot had ever wandered, or if it had, its owner had never brought it back nor told the tale'. Giles, with his passion for voyages and discoveries, an avid reader of anything on the subject from *Robinson Crusoe* to Anson or Cook or the Australian land explorers, found a sympathetic friend in the great botanist, Baron Ferdinand von Mueller, the Victorian Government Botanist, founder of the Melbourne Botanical Gardens and Herbarium, and a notable explorer in his own right; he had begun wandering on his first arrival in South Australia, when he was 23, penetrating the Flinders Ranges as far as Lake Torrens, a very good effort in 1848 for a settler just arrived from Germany. Immensely industrious, kind, generous and enthusiastic, with just enough vanity to remain endearingly comic, von Mueller had long been interested in Giles' passion, an east-west crossing of Australia from the centre. As well as his own exploration in South Australia and Victoria, he had accompanied as naturalist A. C. Gregory's 1855–6 expedition across northern Queensland to the Northern Territory and into Western Australia, and he had been an important member of the committee appointed by the Philosophical Society of Victoria (later the Royal Society) in 1857 'for the purpose of fitting out in Victoria an expedition for traversing the unknown interior of the Australian continent from east to west'. In fact, this expedition turned into the disastrous south–north expedition of Burke and Wills.

Giles' plan was 'to push across the continent from different starting points, upon the Transcontinental Telegraph Line, to the settled districts of Western Australia'. No public money was available, but von Mueller agreed to back Giles privately, and Giles' brother-in-law, G. D. Gill, Samuel Carmichael (a member of the expedition), and Giles himself contributed the remainder of the expenses of fitting out the expedition. It was a tiny affair, just Giles, two white men, a black boy and fifteen horses; compare Burke's caravan of eighteen men, twenty-seven camels, twenty-three horses and twenty-one tons of luggage, backed by £12,000 of public funds. It was twelve years later, but Giles was going on a much more hazardous route.

The dangers and the mysteries were the attraction, rather than hope of reward. Giles was ecstatic at the distances before him. 'There was room for snowy mountains, an inland sea, ancient river, and palmy plain, for races of new kinds of men inhabiting a new and odorous land, for fields of gold and golcondas of gems, for a new flora and a new fauna, and, above all the rest combined, there was room for me!'

III

The First Expedition

GILES and von Mueller decided that the official starting-point of the expedition would be Chambers' Pillar, an extraordinary outcrop of rock discovered by McDouall Stuart near the Finke River some eighty miles north of Charlotte Waters Telegraph Station. Giles of course was a romantic, and so was the good German von Mueller, despite his being one of the most indefatigable and precise classifiers in the history of science, and it was typical of them that their expedition should start at a natural wonder.

Giles made his way across to South Australia from Melbourne, laid in his last supply of stores at Port Augusta on 4 August 1872, and moved at a leisurely pace north up the telegraph line. He was fascinated by the mound springs, those extraordinary pools bubbling with artesian water that rise for hundreds of miles west of Lake Eyre like giant fossilized sea-anemones on the ocean-like plain. The water of most of them is quite fit to drink, if a little aperient. One would swear a bunyip (that monster of Aboriginal mythology) was going to rise from them, when the surface, smooth as an eye surrounded by lashes of reeds, begins to tremble and then tumble into convulsions as the water surges over the edges, and then quietens down again. There are particularly fine ones near one of Giles' halting places at Strangways Springs Telegraph Station; nowadays the roofless stone ruins of the station look as ancient in the immensity around them as a medieval Crusader castle, while the red dust smokes across the track between the sparse mulga and the stubborn saltbush.

At the Peake, a cattle station, Giles had the horses re-shod, and signed on another man, a young fellow called Alec Robinson who cheerily declared that he knew all the country they were about to traverse, and was friendly with all the natives, and promised they would be at the west coast in a couple of weeks. Giles remarks drily: 'I must say he was very good at cooking, and shoeing horses.' Unfortunately the little black boy Dick, or as he liked to call himself, Richard Giles Kew 1872 (having been to school at Kew, near Melbourne), had been subjected to the teasing that anyone in the Australian bush must be prepared for. All up the track people were saying to him: 'By G——, young feller, just you look out when you get *outside*! The wild blacks will (adjective) soon cook you. They'll kill *you* first, you know—they *will* like to cut out your kidney fat! They'll sneak on yer when yer goes out after the horses, they'll have yer and eat yer.'

Poor Dick could not take it, and midway between the Peake and Charlotte Waters, turned tail for home. Now there were only Giles, Carmichael, Robinson, the horses and a little Scotch terrier dog called Monkey.

Giles was pleased to note that Charlotte Waters Telegraph Station, their last outpost of civilization, was called after Lady Charlotte Bacon, the 'Ianthe' to whom Byron dedicated *Childe Harold's Pilgrimage*, a poem which, to judge by the quotations from it in Giles' journals, he must have known by heart. Lady Charlotte, the widow of a brilliant but not altogether honourable cavalry officer, Anthony Bacon, had settled in Adelaide with her children, remaining in South Australia until 1877. In one way or another, poetry has seeded the Australian landscape since its first settlement by

Europeans, even if the crop has not always survived the poor seasons.

By 22 August they had crossed the winding Finke three times, and were in view of Chambers' Pillar across the red sandhills. Their horses were being tortured for the first time by 'that abominable vegetable production, the so-called spinifex or porcupine grass—botanically, the *Triodia*, or *Festuca irritans*'. The bane of all the explorers, whether on horse, camel or foot, spinifex is like a big springy pin cushion, except that the pins all have their points outwards, and the fine brush strokes, green to silvery grey, that rise from its separate round islands on the red sand are the most unmistakable token of the presence of Central Australia. Some of the clumps of spinifex are six feet across, and in the season the grain-like heads (on which stock flourish) are as high as a tall man. Of course, whatever Giles' complaints, spinifex may be a human hazard but it is definitely a natural blessing. Without its millions of islands flatly gripping the red sandy soil, the whole of Central Australia would blow away in red dust.

Giles avoided getting into trouble with the precise von Mueller by the words 'so-called spinifex'. The true spinifex is quite different, the best-known in Australia being *Spinifex hirsutus*, the coast silver grass with spiky heads that roll across the sand with the wind and run onto the water where they drift on the sea standing high on their pale gold spiny rays.

Giles was most impressed by the eighty-foot-high Chambers' Pillar, and immediately found a poetic parallel. 'There it stands, a vast monument of the geological periods that must have elapsed since the mountain ridge, of which it was formerly a part, was washed by the action of old Ocean's waves into mere sandhills at its feet. The stone is so friable that names can be cut in it to almost any depth with a

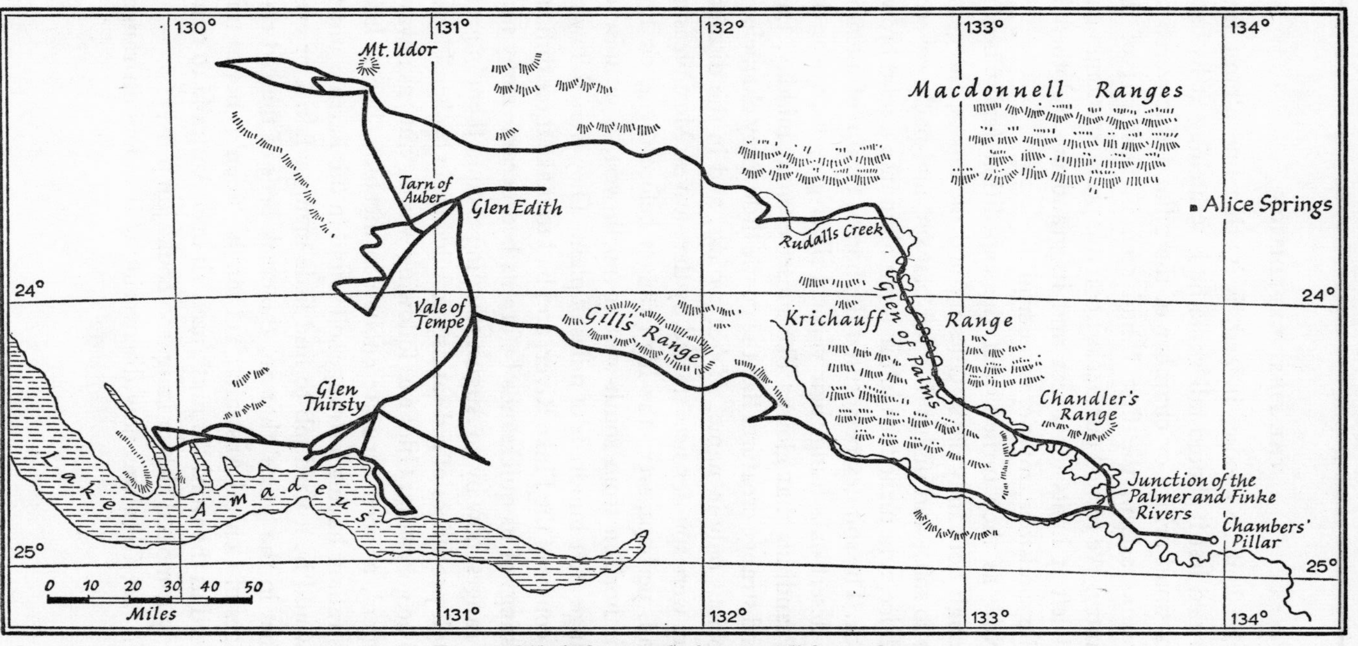

Ernest Giles' first exploring expedition, 1872

pocket-knife: so loose, indeed, is it, that one almost feels alarmed lest it should fall while he is scratching at its base. In a small orifice or chamber of the pillar I discovered an opossum asleep, the first I had seen in this part of the country. We turned our backs upon this peculiar monument, and left it in its loneliness and its grandeur—"clothed in white sandstone, mystic, wonderful"!'

Now as they turned west the expedition really began, through hot sandy days (Giles unshod the horses, the going was so soft), and nights that left blankets and packs covered with ice, and turned tea left in a pannikin into a solid brown block. The spinifex persecuted the horses, groups of splendid tall desert oaks hung their vertical silver-grey hair over the red sandhills that glowed like sunset even at midday, they found strange creatures like the gentle little spiny chameleon, ferocious only in name, *Moloch horridus*, and in the distance there were spinifex fires started by the natives. Most pleasing of all, perhaps, were the high ranges before them, circling their horizon from south-west to north-west, a promise of change after hundreds of miles of plain. They were following the course of the Finke River, and had to make three difficult crossings of its quicksands before its bed became stony near the ranges, now by 30 August standing around them in great rough precipices of red sandstone piled up in broken blocks.

The gorge that Giles was following was for him, as always, a 'glen', a word accurate enough in meaning, but to later Australians having a strange soft sound in this harsh country. It would be a hard job to find little men, or fairies or even rushes in the 'glens' that are the creek beds of the red rock ranges of Central Australia. Yet maybe 'Glen' is not as misplaced as the word 'Mount', used all over Australia to name many a mound that a kangaroo could jump over.

In fact Giles was now discovering real mountain ranges,

even if the mountains themselves had mostly been worn down in the ancient landscape to the level of hills. The Krichauff Range to the north, and the Everard, Musgrave, Mann, Petermann and Rawlinson Ranges to the south, are from two to four thousand feet above sea level, with the highest peak, Mt. Woodroffe, 4,723 ft.

As Giles and his party moved on up the valley, groups of natives gathered on the heights and shouted at them and waved weapons and lit signal fires. More peacefully, there were duck and hundreds of pelicans on the water, and then they came on a totally unexpected specimen, followed by many more, of a giant palm about sixty feet high. Giles' comment in his narrative is a typical mixture of fact and poetry. 'Its dark-hued, dome-shaped frondage contrasted strangely with the paler green foliage of the eucalyptus trees that surrounded it. It was a perfectly new botanical feature to me, nor did I expect to meet it in this latitude. "But there's a wonderful power in latitude, it alters a man's moral relations and attitude." '

They rested on 1 September, it being a Sunday, and the horses very tired from travelling over boulders and stony outcrops along the gorge. Giles climbed a mountain well wooded with native pine, and saw that at last ahead of them there was open country again. He named the mountains the Krichauff Range, but for a while did not know whether to call the Glen after the flowers or the palms. He had never seen more beautiful flowers, their profusion yet another comment on human irrelevance in such regions. 'Why Nature should scatter such floral gems upon such a stony sterile region it is difficult to understand, but such a variety of lovely flowers of every kind and colour I had never met with previously. Nature at times, indeed, delights in contrasts, for here exists a land "where bright flowers are all scentless, and songless bright birds". The flowers alone would have induced me to name this Glen Flora; but having found in it also so many of the stately palm trees, I have called it the Glen of Palms. Peculiar indeed, and romantic too, is this new-found watery glen, enclosed by rocky walls, "Where dial-like, to portion time, the palm-tree's shadow falls".'

The lines from Adam Lindsay Gordon, probably more argued over than any other couplet in Australian literature (Gordon *did* know that there are birds that sing and flowers that have scent in Australia), come from the Dedication at the beginning of *Bush Ballads and Galloping Rhymes*, which had appeared in 1870, on the day before Gordon shot himself. It is interesting that within two years they were part of the essential travelling equipment of an explorer in Central Australia.

By the time the party broke free of the glen it had begun to seem like a prison-house; although about forty miles straight through the ranges, its windings came nearer a hundred, of very rough going. It had rained for about thirty-six hours towards the end of the glen, and Giles had taken the opportunity to plant some of the seeds von Mueller had given him, bestowing on the wilderness cucumbers, melons, 'culinary vegetables' and other plants.

The horses were pleased to be on soft ground again, and the party made good progress beside the Finke and across some of its tributaries, until they were stopped by a wall of mountains and a precipitous gorge, necessitating a change of direction, west-south-west, along a tributary Giles named Rudall's Creek. Giles considered the tessellated pavement of rocks here more beautiful than 'the celebrated Roman one at Bognor'. One of Giles' most pleasant characteristics is his love of nature and animals, even the stars, which constantly fortifies him against the hardships inflicted on him by the same Nature. 'The night was clear and cold; the stars, those sentinels of the sky, appeared intensely bright. To the explorer they must ever be objects of admiration and love, as to them he is indebted for his guidance through the untrodden wilderness he is traversing. "And sweet it is to watch them in the evening skies, weeping dew from their gentle eyes." '

Though driven on by the true explorer's demon, Giles is never in too much of a hurry. 'In the course of my rambles I noticed a great quantity of beautiful flowers upon the hills, of similar kinds to those collected in the Glen of Palms, and these interested me so greatly, that the day passed before I was aware, and I was made to remember the line, "How noiseless falls the foot of Time that only treads on flowers." I saw two kangaroos and one rock wallaby, but they were too wild to allow me to approach near enough to get a shot at them. When I said I walked to-day, I really started on an old favourite horse called Cocky, that had carried me for years, and many a day have I had to thank him for getting me out of difficulties through his splendid powers of endurance. I soon found the hills too rough for a horse, so fixing up his bridle, I said, "Now you stop there till I come back." I believe he knew everything I said, for I used frequently to talk to him. When I came back at night, not thinking he would stay, as the other horses were all feeding within half a mile of him, there he was just as I had left him.'

As they moved further out they came to beautiful grassy plains, and saw numbers of kangaroos and emus, but they were too wild for Giles to get one for the pot, being well hunted by the natives. The flies began to be troublesome; mysteriously in the remotest regions of Central Australia they descend in such clouds that they lie like a repulsive black towel on a man's back, and crawl over each other in heaps to get at the eyes of men and animals. Soon the open plain ceased and they were zigzagging through mulga and then mallee, 'horrible scrubs' that made a journey of a dozen miles take many hours. Robinson and Carmichael made a bad camp while Giles was making a reconnaissance; and they let the horses go without hobbles and lost them, and it took three days to find them all. From this 'wretched dog-hole' of a camp, as Giles observed acidly, 'the only direction in which we could see a yard ahead of us was up towards the sky; and as we were not going that way, it gave us no idea of our next line of route'. By 19 September they were travelling again, but the heat was growing fiercer, and water scarcer and harder to find. They left the creek they had been following, 'to run itself out into some lonely flat or dismal swamp, known only to the wretched inhabitants of this desolate region—over which there seems to brood an unutterable stillness and dread repose'. It was unusual for Giles to be so gloomy about the country. Perhaps he was on edge from the thunderstorm that had been following them, and which now burst in heavy rain which was instantly sucked up by the red sand.

But there was worse to come. When he climbed to the summit of a nearby mount he found they were hemmed in by a confusion of broken rocky ranges, and dense scrub, and that generally it was 'the most gloomy and desolate view imaginable; one, almost enough to daunt the explorer from penetrating any farther into such a dreadful region'.

Giles gives a vivid description, good for tens of thousands of square miles of Australia, of the difficulties of taking pack horses through such scrub. 'It is so dense and thick that in it we cannot see a third of the horses at once; they, of course, continually endeavour to make into it to avoid the stones and triodia; for, generally speaking, the pungent triodia and the mulga acacia appear to be antagonistic members of the vegetable kingdom. The ground in the scrubs is generally soft, and on that account also the horses seek it. Out of kindness, I have occasionally allowed them to travel in the scrubs, when our direct course should have been on the open, until some dire mishap forces us out again; for, the scrubs being so dense, the horses are compelled to crash through them tearing the coverings of their loads, and frequently forcing sticks in between their backs or sides and their saddles, sometimes staking themselves severely. Then we hear a frantic crashing through the scrubs, and the sounds of the pounding of horse-hoofs are the first notice we receive that some calamity has occurred. So soon as we ourselves can force our way through, and collect the horses the best way we can, yelling and howling to one another to say how many each may have got, we discover one or two missing. Then they have to be tracked; portions of loads are picked up here and there, and, in the course of an hour or more, the horse or horses are found, repacked, and on we push again, mostly for the open, through rough and stony spinifex ground, where at least we can see what is going on. These scrubs are really dreadful, and one's skin and clothes get torn and ripped in all directions.'

On 21 September everything went wrong. Giles cut his fingers badly making a hobble peg for the horses; Carmichael and Robinson lost two horses; Giles led the party up a wrong gully. At least there was water in the rock basins in the hills, and in gratitude Giles named the place Mount Udor. After making a solitary and uncomfortable reconnaissance westward, and finding the way still barred by scrub and ranges, Giles decided to withdraw south from 'our prison'. To make things worse for someone so fond of animals, one of the mares foaled, and because of lack of water and the poor condition of the dam the foal had to be killed; 'the mare looked the picture of misery'.

On 1 October they left Mt. Udor, travelling south-south-east and eventually emerging into sandhills and mulga, with yellow everlasting daisies in sheets across the ground. But the lack of water was becoming acute; the horses were suffering severely, and there was only a third of a pint each for the men, which left them too dry to eat anything. Fortunately on the next day, near a cave decorated with aboriginal paintings, Giles found a spring of fresh water. 'No one who has not experienced it, can imagine the pleasure which the finding of such a treasure confers on the thirsty, hungry, and weary traveller; all his troubles for the time are at an end. Thirst, that dire affliction that besets the wanderer in the Australian wilds, at last is quenched; his horses, unloaded, are allowed to roam and graze and drink at will, free from the encumbrance of hobbles, and the traveller's other appetite of hunger is also at length appeased, for no matter what food one may carry, it is impossible to eat it without water. This was truly a mental and bodily relief.'

Resting here for a couple of days, they found many more caves with walls covered in aboriginal drawings and paintings. Giles had almost none of the anthropological curiosity and respect of a Grey or an Eyre. To him native art was simply childish and not to be taken seriously, and those who perpetrated it were 'cave-dwelling, reptile-eating Troglodytes'. 'Mr. Carmichael left upon the walls a few choice specimens of the white man's art, which will help, no doubt, to teach the young native idea, how to shoot either in one direction or another.'

They did not see any natives, but there were smokes everywhere. 'The natives were about, burning, burning, ever burning; one would think they were of the fabled salamander race, and lived on fire instead of water.'

In reconnaissances to the south-west in a big triangle, the horses went 120 miles without water before they returned with relief to the Tarn of Auber, as Giles had called the spring and pool, after Edgar Allan Poe's poem. Carmichael and Giles then rode south on the 11th, and after 55 miles came to a magnificent grassy plain, perhaps 10,000 acres in extent, with enough water for a couple of months for a hundred horses. 'How beautiful is the colour green! What other colour could even Nature have chosen with which to embellish the face of the earth? How, indeed, would red, or blue, or yellow pall upon the eye! But green, emerald green, is the loveliest of all Nature's hues.' These are the words of a thirsty tired man, maybe also remembering his English boyhood. For others, the red sand of Central Australia, with the grey and green of spinifex and mulga, and at the right season (when Giles was there), millions of acres of wild flowers, is one of the wonders of the world. Of course, an emerald green against the red is all the more beautiful. Typically, Giles 'could not resist calling it the Vale of Tempe'. In the far distance he could see 'an exceedingly high and abruptly-ending mountain'.

Giles moved the main camp down towards the grassy plain, and left Alec Robinson there on guard, with Monkey the dog for companion, while he and Carmichael rode to the south-east and south-west exploring the country, making the distant mountain their main objective. 'Alec was a very strange, indeed disagreeable and sometimes uncivil, sort of man; he had found our travels so different from his preconceived ideas, as he thought he was going on a picnic, and he often grumbled and declared he would like to go back again. However, to remain at the camp, with nothing whatever to do and plenty to eat, admirably suited him, and I felt no compunction in leaving him by himself. I would not have asked him to remain if I were in any way alarmed at his position.'

The country they found was pretty desolate, but positively welcoming compared with the enormous salt lake which eventually blocked their passage. Its crust was firm enough for a man to walk on, but totally treacherous for horses. Further to the east they tried to cross again, and nearly lost the horses. 'I made sure they would be swallowed up before our eyes. We were powerless to help them for we could not get near owing to the bog, and we sank up over our knees, where the crust was broken, in hot salt mud. All I could do was to crack my whip to prevent the horses from ceasing to exert themselves, and although it was but a few moments that they were in this danger, to me it seemed an eternity. They staggered at last out of the quagmire, heads, backs, saddles, everything covered with blue mud, their mouths were filled with salt mud also, and they were completely exhausted when they reached firm ground.'

To make life even more unpleasant, it was extremely hot, an almost unbearable 100° at nightfall, and day after waterless day there was still no hope of crossing the salt barrier to the mountain in the distance. Giles wanted to name the lake and the mountain after his patron, von Mueller, but unfortunately the botanist's vanity was not quite up to this, and he insisted Giles call them Lake Amadeus and Mt. Olga, after the King and Queen of Spain, who were patrons of science. Mount Ferdinand and Lake Mueller would have been far more suitable. As a result of von Mueller's European connections, and perhaps snobbery, Central Australia is peppered with German and other European names.

Giles and Carmichael rode a further forty miles to the

west trying to see an end to the lake, but all they had for their pains was a horse frightfully bogged in an arm of the lake. 'We were a hundred miles from the camp, with only one man left there, and sixty-five from the nearest water. I had no choice but to retreat baffled, like Eyre with his Lake Torrens in 1840, at all points.'

The journey back to the nearest water was cruel, with the shade temperature well over 100°. 'Ere the stars had left the sky we were in our saddles again; the horses looked most pitiable objects, their flanks drawn in, the natural vent was distended to an open and extraordinary cavity; their eyes hollow and sunken, which is always the case with horses when greatly in want of water. Two days of such stages will thoroughly test the finest horse that ever stepped. We had thirty-six miles yet to travel to reach the water. The horses being so jaded, it was late in the afternoon when they at last crawled into the little glen; the last few miles being over stones made the pace more slow. Not even their knowledge of the near presence of water availed to inspirit them in the least; probably they knew they would have to wait for hours at the tank, when they arrived, before their cravings for water could be appeased. The thermometer today was 104° in the shade. When we arrived the horses had walked 131 miles without a drink, and it was no wonder that the poor creatures were exhausted.'

While they rested at Glen Thirsty, as Giles called it because they were always in the extremity of thirst when they reached it, he and Carmichael discussed the future of the expedition. They had been three months out, and had not made nearly the progress Giles had hoped for. It was clear that the only way of going on to the west would be by economizing on the stores, and that the only means of accomplishing this was to send Alec Robinson back to Charlotte

Waters. If he was willing to go, then even if Giles and Carmichael had to remain at the camp until January or February, waiting for the rainy season, there still should be enough provisions for them to continue. 'In all these considerations Mr. Carmichael fully agreed, and it was decided that I should inform Alec of our resolution as soon as we returned to camp.'

They found Robinson fit and well at the camp, and Monkey was overjoyed to see them again. Robinson was agreeable to Giles' plan, as long as a watercourse could be found which would take him eastwards to the Finke. In a few days this was achieved, the party discovering some beautiful creeks and pools in which, incredible luxury, it was possible to swim. On the way back to the main camp they had rather an alarming encounter with a number of natives, who seemed very hostile to the idea of anyone else intruding on their hunting grounds and watering places. The men were tall and well made, armed with immensely long spears and woomeras, but they made off when Giles brandished his rifle. 'It seemed as if they knew, or had heard something of white men's ways.' Unlike some other explorers, notably Eyre, Giles does not ever seem particularly ashamed of white men's ways.

They moved out to the east and camped by Stoker's Creek, and there Carmichael delivered a fatal blow to the expedition, by telling Giles that he was returning to base with Robinson. 'Of course I could not control him; he was a volunteer, and had contributed towards the expenses of the expedition. We had never fallen out, and I thought he was as ardent in the cause of exploration as I was, so that when he informed me of his resolve it came upon me as a complete surprise. My arguments were all in vain; in vain I showed how, with the stock of provisions we had, we might keep the field for months. I even offered to retreat to the Finke, so that we should not have such arduous work for want of water, but it was all useless.

'It was with distress that I lay down on my blankets that night, after what he had said. I scarcely knew what to do. I had yet a lot of horses heavily loaded with provisions; but to take them out into a waterless, desert country by myself, was impossible.'

There was nothing for it but to retreat to the Telegraph Line. The party moved off again, everyone silent. Later in the day Giles rode up the narrow valley of a small creek. He saw a few natives, but was not worried, until suddenly he found himself at the end of a narrow gorge, with cliffs all around, and on the cliffs a crowd of natives all with their spears towards him. 'Both parties seemed paralyzed by the appearance of the other.' Yearning for water, Giles determined to brave the thing out, fortifying himself with a quatrain of poetry.

Cowards, 'tis said, in certain situations
Derive a sort of courage from despair;
And then perform, from downright desperation,
Much bolder deeds than many a braver man would dare.

He managed to get a few mouthfuls of water, then mounted slowly facing the natives, and suddenly wheeled his horse around and galloped full tilt out of the cul-de-sac, with spears rattling on the rocks around him. He reached the other members of the party safely, but greetings were hardly comradely. 'Upon rejoining my companions, as we now seldom spoke to one another, I merely told them I had seen water and natives, but that it was hardly worth while to go back to the place, but that they could go if they liked. Robinson asked me why I had ridden my horse West

Australian—shortened to W.A., but usually called Guts, from his persistent attention to his "inwards"—so hard when there seemed no likelihoods of our getting any water for the night? I said, "Ride him back and see." '

In this stiff atmosphere, at least Nature turned kindly, as their next camp was by a big pool where they caught all the fish they could eat. Then by easy stages they came to the junction of the Palmer and Finke rivers, and so back to the Telegraph Line.

Towards the end, Giles sent Robinson and Carmichael on ahead, and he himself reached Charlotte Waters on 1 December 1872. 'My expedition was over. I had failed certainly in my object, . . . but not through any fault of mine.'

But more bitter news still was waiting at Charlotte Waters. Colonel Peter Egerton Warburton was there, with a strong expedition sponsored by (Sir) Thomas Elder and Captain Hughes, and he had news of another expedition under W. C. Gosse, sponsored by the South Australian Government, both with the same aim as Giles, to cross the continent. Moreover, both expeditions were equipped with camels. It seemed that the South Australians were jealous of the Victorian-sponsored expedition of Giles, and were determined to beat him to the West.

There was nothing dog-in-the-manger about Giles. He gave Colonel Warburton and his son all the information they asked, and showed them his map, and sold them some of his equipment. But they and Gosse had other ideas, and were both leaving from Alice Springs, in the Macdonnell Ranges.

IV

The Second Expedition

It is nearly a hundred years since Giles first penetrated beyond the red splendours of the South Australian and Northern Territory ranges into the Western Australian desert that he called after Alfred Gibson who died there in 1874. Yet there are still natives in these regions who have only recently seen white men for the first time, and it is still all too easy to die there. Apart from the meteorological station at Giles on the edge of the Rawlinson Range, a couple of missions, a few cattle stations and thousands of tourists dashing in to Ayers Rock and Mt. Olga and out again, there is still no settlement for a thousand miles between the old Telegraph Line and the tiny town of Wiluna in Western Australia.

The man who probably knows as much as any white man about that country is Len Beadell, who spent more than three years in the 1960's making the first east–west road (of the simple sort typical of Central Australia) from the Adelaide–Alice Springs road to Carnegie station, 400 miles from Kalgoorlie. His judgments on the country are worth listening to, especially as he very nearly lost his life in Gibson's Desert, with a Land-Rover, in the second half of the twentieth century.

Beadell writes in his *Too Long in the Bush*: 'The country of Central Australia can be divided up into four types, sand ridges covered with thick mulga scrub, sand ridges among mountain ranges, sand ridges covered with spinifex, and bare sand ridges.

'Bordering the northern edge of the Nullarbor Plain are the sand ridges covered with mulga. These extend for five hundred miles east to west without a break, and the belt is two hundred miles wide. The ridges are parallel, often only fifty yards apart, and a single ridge can be a hundred miles long. They average forty feet in height, and their southern face is the steeper. Travelling from north to south is almost feasible, therefore, whereas in most instances the reverse is impossible except on foot. The mulga trees are up to twelve feet high, casting about twenty per cent shade, and are extremely old for their size, being hardy enough to survive each five-month-long scorching summer.

'During a drought in the cattle country, where mulga is often found, stock can live on the herbage. Here and there are small patches, not more than a mile across, of she-oak, indicating the sure presence of a limestone ground surface in that area, which in turn means higher country. This region is also relieved by occasional salt lakes, varying in size from very small to many miles in diameter. Very close to these, the regular pattern of the sand ridges is disturbed; they are converted into confused mountains of sand which are very often quite bare and move about with the wind. The lakes are mostly bottomless blue mud with a thin coating of white salt, and must be avoided at all costs. I was hopelessly bogged for a week at a time during my early contacts with them, as they look so invitingly smooth after months of pushing over sandhills and through dense mulga.'

Beadell describes the climate of this 'most heart-breaking section of Australia' as follows: 'From November to March it is searingly hot and dry; April, June, and July have ideal temperatures but it is dry; August and September are dry with seemingly never-ending winds, and it appears to be fairly dry in October. It might be a little unjust to say it is all that dry, because for some years we have had up to two inches of rain. After a cycle of about twelve years, six inches can be expected. But clear skies will be seen for most of the year. To quote one small boy's answer to an examination question, "The climate of Central Australia in summer is such that its inhabitants have to live elsewhere."

'The unpleasantness of even a slight contact with a blanket has forced me to get up around midnight and try to cool down with a wet cloth, and even then the temperature has been over the century. I know I wished I were elsewhere.'

Not only Len Beadell, but anyone who has travelled even to the fringe of 'this most heart-breaking section of Australia' will have no reservations in admiring the courage and tenacity of men like Giles, who went back there again and again.

Though dismayed at the entrance of the Warburton and Gosse expeditions into his territory, particularly 'as my chances of competing with them would be small indeed, as I could only command horses, and was not then known to Sir Thomas Elder, the only gentleman in Australia who possessed camels', Giles immediately telegraphed von Mueller asking for support for a second expedition. The Baron speedily applied pressure to his wealthy Victorian friends, while Giles asked the South Australian Government for some assistance, in return for all the information he was able to hand over from his first expedition. However, Sir Henry Ayers and his Government already had their man, Gosse, in the field, and they only very grudgingly agreed to give some support for Giles, to the extent of £250, on condition that the money was spent on fresh explorations, and that Giles gave the S.A. Government a copy of the map and journal of his expedition. Giles comments, 'My poverty, and not my will, consented to accept so mean a gift.'

Of course to Giles, totally insulated by sand and mulga from the outside world for three and a half months, the meeting with Warburton had been a complete shock. But in fact there had already been friendly contact between von Mueller, Elder and the South Australian Government. On 24 September 1872 von Mueller had written to Elder suggesting that Gosse's expedition which was to leave from the Macdonnell Ranges, should 'turn in the direction of Lake Barlee' (in north-western Western Australia). 'It would then cross Mr. Giles' supposed or intended track only on one place, and as it has also the superiority of using Dromedaries it might well endeavour to return from Lake Barlee to Stuart's range after refitting in Western Australia.' Von Mueller says he 'would like to get Gosse's plants', and that Warburton had already kindly promised his.

Von Mueller had also written to the South Australian Government on behalf of Giles. 'Kindly remember that poor Giles had set his all in the world on his own enterprise, and that this undertaking at my original suggestion seems to have led to that proposed by Thomas Elder. In the interest of the poor man who is without camels and most slenderly equipped I trust that any new expedition from your colony will not adopt the same line as that of Giles and his companions.'

Warburton was already an old man, by exploring standards. There must have been some criticism of this, for on 15 August 1872 (Sir) Thomas Elder sent a note to the Hon. Henry Ayers (Premier of South Australia): 'My dear Sir,

Colonel Warburton is only 58 years of age *this very day*.'

Actually he was 59, and his birthday was on the 12th, but to Elder the Colonel was *only* 58. Warburton had been a

Artesian Mound Springs, Central Australia; periodic water upheaval

Baron Ferdinand von Mueller

Richard Egerton Warburton, Colonel Peter Egerton Warburton and J. W. Lewis

sailor, and then a soldier in the Bombay Army for 24 years. He left India to emigrate to New Zealand, but liked Adelaide so much that he left the ship there in 1853, and later was appointed Commissioner of Police. He made a number of exploring journeys to the west and north of South Australia, the old Indian soldier taking to the burning outback like a salamander. However, the deserts of Western Australia were to be infinitely worse than anything Warburton had ever experienced, and it was a miracle that he ever reached the West, even after leaving a trail of camel bones behind him.

His party consisted of three white men besides himself, including his son Richard and an experienced bushman, J. W. Lewis, with an Aboriginal, and two Afghans; they were equipped with 21 camels, later reduced to 17. They left Alice Springs on 15 April 1873, Warburton's instructions being vaguely 'to explore the country between Central Mount Stuart and the settled districts of Western Australia'. He headed west to begin with, but gradually in the search for water moved more and more to the north until after 106 days, and after riding 1,700 miles, he was only 50 miles closer to Perth than he had been at Alice Springs. On the fringes of the Great Sandy Desert he pitched camp at a native well he christened Waterloo Wells, and there he and the party stayed for 56 days, defeated in every direction from north-west to south, until Lewis found some water to the north-west. This long halt severely reduced his supply of provisions.

Residence in India and Australia had not made the aristocratic Colonel into a humanitarian. His method of finding native wells was to capture an Aborigine and make him (or her) lead the party to the precious water. Of course this water was also precious to the Aborigines, and one can imagine the terror and resentment inspired in them by these white strangers, and their monstrous beasts. One day they captured a young native woman, 'a great triumph', but 'the creature escaped by gnawing through a thick hair rope with which she was fastened to a tree'. On another day they captured 'a howling hideous old hag. We secured this witch by tying her thumbs behind her back and haltering her by the neck to a tree. She howled all night and we had to watch her by turns or she would have got away also. There is no way of securing these creatures if you take your eyes off them for ten minutes.' The next day they let her go. 'She had been of no use to us and her sex alone saved her from punishment, for, under pretence of leading us to some native wells, she took us backwards and forwards over heavy sand-hills, exhausting the camels and my small stock of patience.'

A year after leaving Adelaide, Warburton was still in the West Australian deserts, losing camels, travelling by night to avoid the heat (and thus achieving little in the way of exploration), till on 12 December 1873, after nearly perishing on several occasions, he sent Lewis ahead with two camels to try to reach the station on the De Grey river. Lewis took a letter from Warburton to Thomas Elder. 'We are all alive, and that is all. We have lost everything, and have only two camels left out of seventeen. Our journey has been difficult beyond all I had supposed possible. We are reduced to such a state by famine that we can scarcely crawl 100 yards, and are quite incapable of hard work, or indeed any work at all. . . . We are gaunt pictures of suffering, and have nothing but the few rags we stand up in.' On 29 December Lewis returned with help; they were saved, though Warburton had lost the sight of one eye, his son was a sick man and, 'Saleh the Afghan left his finger in Roeburne'.

On their eventual return to Adelaide the South Australian Legislative Assembly voted Warburton £1,000, and £500 to be divided amongst other members of the party. Warburton was awarded the Gold Medal of the Royal Geographical Society, and the Queen made him a C.M.G. He paid a short visit to England to see his aged mother, found the climate 'insupportable', and returned to Adelaide, where he died in 1889.

There is something both gallant and absurd about leathery old Warburton, perhaps symbolized by the occasion on 28 November 1863, when he trod on a snake in the moonlight. 'It turned upon me, of course, but whether it bit my trousers or not I don't know; if it did, I derived some advantage from my extra thinness, as it could not find the leg inside them.' Warburton's adventures were so extraordinary, so extreme, that some years after they were published in London in 1875, they caught the eye of that novelist *par excellence* of romantic adventure, Jules Verne, who based a novel, *Mistress Branican*, upon them.

Warburton's expedition, which Giles farewelled at Charlotte Waters in November 1872, succeeded in reaching the Indian Ocean but otherwise was disastrous. The other party, under W. C. Gosse, failed in its objective but came to no mishap. It was officially sponsored by the South Australian Government and generously supplied with camels by Thomas Elder and Walter M. Hughes, at their own expense, and it left Alice Springs on 21 April 1873, consisting of four white men, three Afghans and a black boy. William Christie Gosse was born in England in 1842, and was an officer of the S.A. Survey Department, under that remarkable man G. W. Goyder. He was chosen as leader of the east–west expedition, at £500 a year, and for some mysterious reason ordered to start from Alice Springs. The original plan was for him to start from Charlotte Waters, and thus be 200 miles south of Warburton, but perhaps it was thought better that he should be nearer Warburton's tracks than those of Giles. Certainly he had the benefit of Giles' discoveries, maps and information before leaving.

Thus it is all the more puzzling that, after heading west, he turned south and made for Giles' Mt. Udor, Glen Edith and Lake Amadeus. The only explanation he gives is that repeated reconnaissances to the west revealed nothing but waterless country; but that surely was the challenge for which he had camels and provisions. Travelling south he reached Ayers Rock and named it; 'it is the most wonderful natural feature I have ever seen.' He was then the first white man to visit Giles' Mt. Olga, to poor Giles' eternal mortification, and he then moved west and south-west to the Mann Range; 'the waters here had every appearance of being permanent and the country equal to anything in the north.' As Forrest observed, coming the other way in 1874, 'it must have been a good season'.

However, when he made a reconnaissance on horses west of his Depot 14 at Mt. Cooper he discovered nothing but sandhills and dry rocky ranges. He reached and named Mount Squires and the Townsend Range, and turned back, his horses wretched from lack of water. 'I have pushed on as far as it is safe,' he wrote, but he did not explain why he did not attempt to push on further with camels. He reached the Telegraph Line again safely on 19 December 1873, having been out 226 days. Gosse, the professional surveyor, 31 years old, tough and experienced, with excellent men, camels and horses, and a good season, was the most cautious of all the explorers of this region of sand and spinifex and no water. Ironically enough, he was only 39 when he died.

In 1874 a party from the West, led by John Forrest (later Premier of Western Australia and holder of various Ministerial posts in the first Federal Parliament), succeeded by splendid daring in crossing this terrible country with horses only, to the comparative safety of the Warburton Range. The explorer's point of crisis, whether to go on or back, was reached by Forrest at Blyth Creek, longitude 125° 27′ East, where he was based for seventeen days in July and August 1874 at good water, making reconnaissances to the east. Giles' furthest west in November 1873 was at longitude 125° 37′ East. 'At this point I returned. Unless I was prepared to go a hundred or more miles, ten, fifteen or twenty in such a region would be of no use.' He did not know he was less than ten miles from the good water at Blyth Creek. He was alone, with one exhausted horse, in temperatures well over the century. Forrest, in winter, with a strong party, decided to go on. 'We are now in the very country that had driven Mr. Gosse back. (I have since found it did the same for Mr. Giles.) No time is to be lost. I am determined to make the best use of the time, if only the water will last, and to keep on searching. (Even now, months after the time, sitting down writing this journal, I cannot but recall my feelings of anxiety at this camp.)' So, on the finest margins, does this country let one man through and drive another back.

Forrest had originally submitted his plan for crossing from the West to the Telegraph Line to Governor Weld in July 1872, when at the age of 25 he was already an experienced explorer. The Western Australian Legislative voted the £400 Forrest had asked for, but with Warburton, Gosse and Giles already in the field Weld decided that Forrest should wait and see what happened to the three other explorers, when he would also have the benefit of their discoveries. The decision was both shrewd and well-mannered; only twelve years before there had been the atmosphere of a race about the McDouall Stuart and Burke and Wills expeditions, and the South Australian camels were already racing against

Giles' Victorian-backed horses. With any luck, the Western Australians might stand back in dignity and then quietly conquer the field; and this is what they did.

By the end of January 1873 Giles was back in Adelaide recruiting men and equipment for his Second Expedition. His old friend Tietkens came over from Melbourne to join him, and he also signed up a young man called Jimmy Andrews. Early in March they left Adelaide with a light four-wheeled trap and several horses, buying more as they went north; Giles sold the wagon to the Bagot brothers when he reached the Peake; he now had twenty pack-horses and four riding horses, two little dogs, and a new man. 'Here a short young man accosted me, and asked me if I did not remember him, saying at the same time that he was "Alf". I fancied I knew his face, but thought it was at the Peake that I had seen him, but he said, "Oh no, don't you remember Alf with Bagot's sheep at the north-west bend of the Murray? my name's Alf Gibson, and I want to go out with you." I said, "Well, can you shoe? can you ride? can you starve? can you go without water? and how would you like to be speared by the blacks outside?" He said he could do everything I had mentioned, and he wasn't afraid of the blacks. He was not a man I would have picked out of a mob, but men were scarce, and as he seemed so anxious to come, and as I wanted somebody, I agreed to take him.'

Giles had decided to make his start this time from Ross's Water-hole in the Alberga, at its junction with the Stevenson, and head north-west from there straight to Mt. Olga, which so long had beckoned to him across the bottomless, glaring salt crust of Lake Amadeus. This time he would be well south of the lake. The expedition left the Alberga after some days of rain, on 4 August 1873.

The going was fairly easy, and although after a few days

they came on bunches of their old enemy the spinifex, there were compensations like the very pretty native poplar, a tree so regular and elegant, with its pale green fluttering leaves, that it looks as if it had been planted in a garden. There were also diversions such as the dead tree supporting the tarpaulin making shade for their dinner, that fell down on the head of Jimmy Andrews, which broke the tree, half of it then falling on Giles' back; 'as it only fell on Jimmy's head, of course it couldn't hurt him.' The country became more open, and even on occasions feasted the horses with green grass. Then there was a valley with that pure, idyllic beauty only to be found in remote places, nowhere more so than in Central Australia, where no sound of human being or animal distracts the echo of a bird-call. The Central Australian birds have slow, deliberate calls, with an extraordinary roundness of tone; anyone who has been in those regions, whisked blindfolded back there again by a magician would instantly know where he was. One bird leisurely whistles the letters IS of the Morse Code (.. ...) on the one note; another goes three notes down the scale, misses the fourth, and finishes on the fifth. Surrounded by song in the valley, Giles immediately found a poetic reference. 'The atmosphere seemed cleared of all grossness or impurities, a few sunlit clouds floated in space, and a perfume from Nature's own laboratory was exhaled from the flowers and vegetation around. It might well be said that here were

Gusts of fragrance on the grasses,
In the skies a softened splendour;
Through the copse and woodland passes
Songs of birds in cadence tender.

'The country was so agreeable here we had no desire to traverse it at railway speed; it was delightful to loll and lie upon the land, in abandoned languishment beneath the solar ray.'

Beyond the valley towards the distant ranges it was beautiful in a different way, the beauty of the red sand ridges covered with flowers, unbelievably thick and close as in a spring Swiss meadow, against the gigantic round rocks and slabs of stone that are hurled together and change from red to blue to purple according to the angle of the light. Of all the Central Australian explorers Giles is the one who realized the beauty of the country, which now draws thousands of tourists and supports an industry of Aboriginal painters.

The spirit of the good Baron von Mueller was always with Giles, and in amongst the profusion of native flowers and shrubs Giles planted the seeds sent from the Melbourne herbarium, Tasmanian blue gum, wattle, melons, pumpkins, cucumbers, maize and more. These particular seeds may have been rather ambitious for such country, but the Baron was a scientist of genius who saw what the future could bring to the dry country. 'Other generations', he wrote in a letter in 1874, 'will see marvellous changes in these supposed deserts by the dissemination of perennial grasses, clovers, lucerne, and numerous other fodder herbs, and by draining into permanent basins the moisture which now, after occasional rainfalls, so rapidly evaporates.' He goes on to lament the opportunities being wasted of planting Australian acacias and eucalypti in the African deserts; he would be happy could he see the millions of them now growing from Libya to South Africa.

Giles was so carried away by 'the singular and almost awful beauty' of the ranges and the 'grassy glades' of the plains that he made a startling leap in his narrative from Central Australia to half a page of rough rhymes printed as prose, on the subject of Merrie England and Sherwood

Forest. However, there was one vital difference from the England of running streams. There was very little water to be found in the Ayers Range, as Giles called this upheaval of rocks, 'huge red, rounded solid blocks of stone, shaped like the backs of enormous turtles'.

As usual, Aboriginal cave paintings in the ranges did not please him. He was a true Victorian believer in Progress and Religion, and it was bad luck for the Aborigines that they had been placed by God at the bottom of the ladder. 'Upon the opposite or eastern side of this rock was a large ledge or cave, under which the Troglodytes of these realms had frequently encamped. It was ornamented with many of their rude representations of creeping things, amongst which the serpent class predominated; there were also other hideous shapes, of things such as can exist only in their imaginations, and they are but the weak endeavours of these benighted beings to give form and semblance to the symbolisms of the dread superstitions, that, haunting the vacant chambers of their darkened minds, pass amongst them in the place of either philosophy or religion.'

The journey went on through the rocks and flowers of this extraordinary country, Giles' solitary reconnaissances giving him time to consider the true effect of loneliness on the human being, for he was well aware that Byron and his other favourite poets, those singers of the delights of solitude, had never been, as he was now, more than a thousand miles away from the nearest town. 'Nothing could appal the mind so much as the contemplation of eternal solitude . . . for human sympathy is one of the passions of human nature.' So he thought as he watched his horse munching away, 'up to his eyes in the most magnificent herbage'. And later, in the cold morning, with the thermometer at 28°, he quoted Byron for breakfast.

The next day, 30 August, he returned to the place where he had left the party, but found that Tietkens had ridden over to better water a few miles away. As it was Tietkens' 29th birthday, Giles called this pleasant spot Tietkens' Birthday Creek. Following the creek up later, they found a large and enchanting natural amphitheatre, complete with that rarest of natural blessings in Central Australia, a fast flowing stream, in ponds of which they shot wild duck for dinner. 'This was really a delightful discovery. Everything was of the best kind here—timber, water, grass and mountains. In all my wanderings, over thousands of miles in Australia, I never saw a more delightful and fanciful region than this, and one indeed where a white man might live and be happy.' Of course it had to be called a Glen, and Giles named both Glen and Creek Ferdinand, after Baron von Mueller.

However, this paradise launched them into a very alarming encounter with a large number of natives, who loosed volleys of jagged, ten-foot spears at them. Giles got the horses together and fired a few shots into the branches over the natives' heads. This did not scare them for long, and soon the spears were flying again. Giles and the party replied with their full armoury of two rifles, two shot guns and five revolvers, firing just short of the attackers so the sand and stones flew up into their faces. 'In consequence of our not shooting any of them, they began to jeer and laugh at us, slapping their backsides at and jumping about in front of us, and indecently daring and deriding us. These were evidently some of those lewd fellows of the baser sort (Acts xii. 5).'

Giles drove the fresh attack off by firing amongst them; he writes as if he did not wound any of them. His conscience was not much troubled by feelings of guilt. 'It is next to impossible in Australia for an explorer to discover excellent and well-watered regions without coming into deadly conflict with the aboriginal inhabitants. The aborigines are always the aggressors, but then the white man is a trespasser in the first instance, which is a cause sufficient for any atrocity to be committed upon him.'

But other explorers, Eyre above all, had proved that the Aborigines only attacked because they, earlier on, had been attacked themselves. It is significant that Giles heard one of the leaders of this group call out in English 'Walk, white fellow, walk,' indicating that they were not wild blacks who had seen no white men.

The next day, moving on peacefully, Giles found another valley that he pronounced even more beautiful than the last. He was particularly entranced by the carpet of grass and flowers, mostly the glorious deep magenta and rose and pink of parakeelya, whose large cups of flowers over little fleshy leaves are not only beautiful but excellent feed for stock; there are records of animals travelling three hundred miles without water, living off parakeelya.

So much of Australian exploration is a dour, hard business of blackened throats and reddened eyes that it is a joy to read of an explorer innocently happy in what he has discovered, and devoid of all that pseudo-toughness often thought obligatory in those outsiders who go into the Australian outback. There was no tougher bushman than Giles; and there he is, 'certain it is the most charming and romantic spot I ever shall behold. . . . I would not have missed finding such a spot, upon—I will not say what consideration.' And what does this sweaty horseman call this romantic spot?—'The Fairies' Glen'!

Giles was well aware that the signs of occupation around the Glen were not left by fairies. The Aborigines were not there at the time, to spoil his romantic dream with shriek and spear, but he saw their presence and his own in the context of divine progress, prepared to accept the possibility of himself and his kind being driven from the earth by 'another race of yet unknown beings, of an order infinitely higher, infinitely more beloved, than we. On me, perchance, the eternal obloquy of the execution of God's doom may rest, for being the first to lead the way, with prying eye and trespassing foot, into regions so fair and so remote; but being guiltless alike in act or intention to shed the blood of any human creature, I must accept it without a sigh.'

Walking through the hills with Tietkens in the morning he saw a high bare rock over which water was gushing, 'like a monstrous diamond hung in mid-air', and he called this summit Mount Oberon, and allowed himself to imagine some future time when there would be flocks and herds and large centres of population in the rich valleys amongst these mountains, now called (after Gosse's name) the Musgrave Range. Here it seemed that the explorer's dream might at last come true, though these explorers knew well enough what the country behind them might turn into in drought. As Tietkens puts it: 'But few can enter into the joys and anticipations or sympathize with the anxieties and hours of suspense of the Explorer and Pioneer; still the life of such men is in their hands and is not counted of much value by themselves and still less no doubt by an Insurance Agent; always, always hopeful under the most trying and dreadful conditions, one never knows but over the next hills the change may come, and reveal rivers of water, luxuriant herbage and noble forests. We sighted the Musgrave Ranges after a pleasant ramble of 200 miles that was, owing to the late rains, quite a pleasure trip; very vastly different this 200 miles would be under other circumstances, for in a month's time every drop of water would have disappeared, and to retrace our steps had we desired it, would have been a task of more than ordinary difficulty.'

And now, from another hill, Giles' prime target, Mt. Olga, was in view, still many miles away. From this hill he could also see that the Musgrave Ranges ran on to the west, and then, broken and parted, it rose again into high points, called by Giles the Bowen Range, but now called the Mann Range, for as it turned out Gosse had got there first and as in many cases, his names were kept and Giles' not used. They pushed on across poor country, cheered only by the handsome desert oaks, the most elegant of the casuarinas.

On 14 September they reached Mt. Olga, sought so long and so close across the Lake. Mt. Olga, with Ayers Rock so different close by, is one of the wonders of the world, its bare humps crowding together, rising 1,500 feet sheer from the plain, and covering an area of 25 square miles. Giles did his rather floundering best to describe it, while admitting that was impossible. 'The appearance of this mountain is marvellous in the extreme, and baffles an accurate description . . . it is formed of several vast and solid, huge, and rounded blocks of bare red conglomerate stones, being composed of untold masses of rounded stones of all kinds and sizes, mixed like plums in a pudding, and set in vast and rounded shapes upon the ground. Water was running from the base, down a stony channel, filling several rocky basins. The water disappeared in the sandy bed of the creek, where the solid rock ended. I made an attempt to climb a portion of this singular mound, but the sides were too perpendicular; I could only get up about 800 or 900 feet, on the front or lesser mound; but without kites and ropes, or projectiles, or wings, or balloons, the main summit is unscalable.'

Enchanted as Giles was with the extraordinary presence of Mt. Olga, he was not free to admire it in peace. An appalling shock was awaiting him, in the shape of the marks of a wagon and horses, and the softer tracks of camels. They could mean nothing else than the fact that Gosse had been there before him. 'Had the earth yawned at my feet, for ever separating me from this mountain, or had another of similar appearance risen suddenly before my eyes, I could have not been more astonished at the sight; for I knew Mr. Gosse had left the Telegraph-line many hundreds of miles to the north of my starting point. . . . I was not only astonished—I had reason to be annoyed as well—because, as the Government Expedition had come down to the mountain, and was now travelling in advance of me, on the only line of country that seemed traversable—that is to say—along the line of range now lying south and south-westward from here, it had probably more than a month's start of me. I was compelled to reflect, of what earthly use it was for me to continue in the same region with another explorer ahead. I had thoughts of returning immediately and throwing up my expedition at once.'

Giles moved camp to softer ground, and they enjoyed a swim in one of the many rocky basins that lie in the little streams which run between the great cliffs of Mt. Olga in good seasons. Away to the east he could see 'a high and solitary mound', actually the biggest rock in the world, already named by Gosse Ayers Rock after the South Australian Premier. Amidst such grand surroundings it was impossible for a man of Giles' temperament to think of turning back. Instead, it gave him all the more impetus to go on into the wilderness. 'I thought I was the monarch of all I surveyed and the lord of the fowl and the brute; but lo! a greater than I is here. So I must depart to some remoter spot where none shall dispute my sway. I first, however, determined that I would overtake Mr. Gosse and have a friendly intercourse; then we might agree to differ in our lines of march.'

After a rest they set off in the direction of the Mann Range, which despite some dry intervals, gave them 'a most picturesque and delightful bath' in a cascade Giles christened Zoe's Glen. In another valley, on 28 September, the horses suddenly started sniffing the ground, and from the freshness of Gosse's dray tracks, which Giles had been following, he realized that the horses were scenting the camels. Not far away the hills to the north receded, and a beautiful plain came into view, 'level as a billiard table and green as an emerald'. Giles' imagination immediately leaped into action, with a result astonishing enough to be reminiscent of Dr. Johnson's verdict on the wit of the Metaphysical poets: 'a discovery of occult resemblances in things apparently unlike. . . . The most heterogeneous ideas are yoked by violence together; nature and art are racked for illustrations, comparisons, and allusions.' 'I could not help thinking what a glorious spot this would make for the display of cavalry manœuvres. In my neutral eye I could see

The rush of squadrons sweeping,
Like whirlwinds o'er the plain;

and mentally hear

The shouting of the slayers,
The screeching of the slain.

I called this splendid circle the Champ de Mars.'

What Giles' imagination had not revealed to him was that Gosse was retreating homewards, heading east, not west as Giles thought. In fact, around 30 September the two parties were less than 30 miles apart; when Giles left his camp at the Champ de Mars, and crossed the Western Australian border, Gosse was at Moses Creek, resting before striking north-east to the Tomkinson Range.

A few days later, on 5 October, Giles halted amid the black-streaked bastions of the Cavenagh Range, christening his camp Fort Mueller. The next day, on the lower grassy ground, he struck Gosse's tracks again and was startled to find that the tracks were heading east. For some mysterious reason, which Giles did not waste his energies in trying to solve, Gosse had given up.

Giles went on, but a few days later, from a hill in waterless country, the view ahead 'to a traveller in any way predisposed to retrace his steps would at once put a stop to any further progress westward'. It was a mass of hideous scrubby gullies and ridges, and crossing it later they fortunately found water; as they shod the horses there, Giles called it the Shoeing Camp. The only compensation was the finding of eggs in some of the enormous nests of that strange bird the mallee-hen or lowan, incubators made of sand and sticks and leaves, sometimes six feet high and a hundred feet in circumference. 'We thanked Providence for supplying us with such luxuries in such a wilderness. There are much easier feats to perform than the carrying of lowans' eggs, and for the benefit of any readers who don't know what those eggs are like, I may mention that they are larger than a goose egg, and of a more delicious flavour than any other egg in the world. Their shell is beautifully pink tinted, and so terribly fragile that, if a person is not careful in lifting them, the fingers will crunch through the tinted shell in an instant. Therefore, carrying a dozen of such eggs is no easy matter. I took upon myself the responsibility of bringing our prize safe into camp, and I accomplished the task by packing them in grass, tied up in a handkerchief, and slung round

Mount Olga, from sixty miles to the west, from *Australia Twice Traversed*

William Ernest Powell Giles

William Henry Tietkens

my neck; a fine fardel hanging on my chest immediately under my chin.'

With Fort Mueller as a main depot, and the Shoeing Camp as a forward camp, Giles stayed in the area for more than three months, making wearisome thrusts west, south, north, and finally leaving, striking north from Fort Mueller. It was hard work, for although Tietkens was an excellent companion and a reliable second-in-command, both Gibson and Jimmy Andrews were amiable but stupid. Jimmy would do things like setting fire to the spinifex near the camp on a windy day, nearly destroying everything. He also had some very curious habits. 'Jimmy and I and the two dogs were at the camp. He had the habit of biting the dogs' noses, and it was only when they squealed that I saw what he was doing; today Cocky was the victim. I said, "What the deuce do you want to be biting the dog's nose for, you might seriously injure his nasal organ?" "Horgin," said Jimmy, "do you call his nose a horgin?" I said, "Yes, any part of the body of man or animal is called an organ." "Well," he said, "I never knew that dogs carried horgins about with them before." I said, "Well, they do, and don't you go biting any of them again." Jimmy of course, my reader can see, was a queer young fellow.'

On 9 November, on one of these reconnaissances, Giles decided to make one last attempt on his own to find water to the west for the whole party. Sending Gibson and Jimmy back to the Shoeing Camp, he gave his horse a last drink, fixed a leather waterbag holding eight gallons up a tree to see him back to safety, and rode away west alone, 'like knight errant on sad adventure bound, though unattended by any esquire or shield-bearer'. Soon the red sand ridges gave way to burnt, gravelly, level ground covered with the savage spinifex. He found a native well with some putrid water in

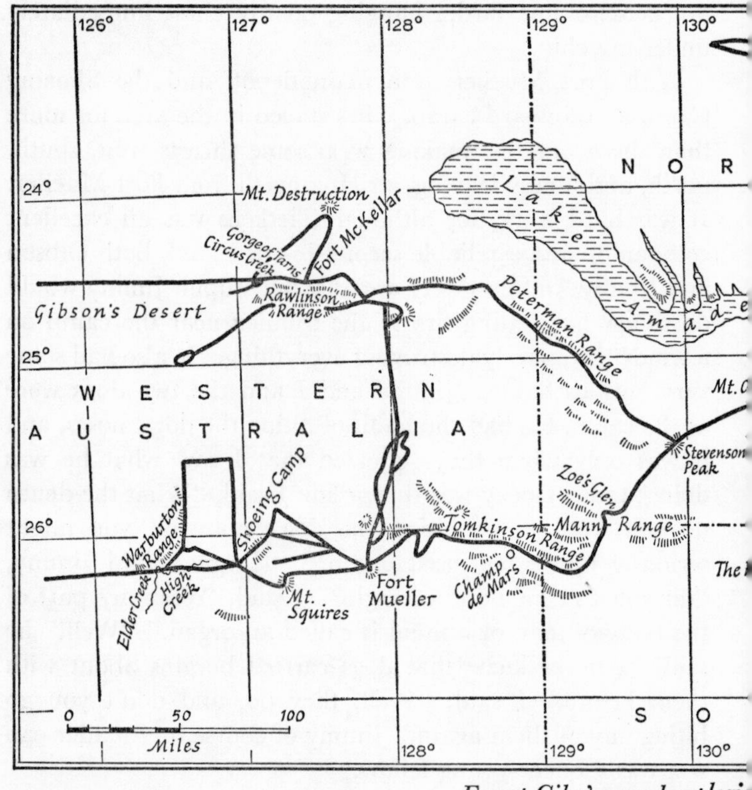

Ernest Giles' second explori

it that even the thirsty horse could not manage, and then continued out into the desert until he was at 125° 37′, 50 miles from his waterbag in the tree, and 90 miles from the Shoeing Camp. It seemed to him impossible to go on; his horse was done in, the near-desert was unchanging, there might be no water for 150 miles. How he longed for a camel! He was not to know that Forrest's Blyth Creek was only 10 miles away.

He turned back, and the stinking pit saved his horse. 'It

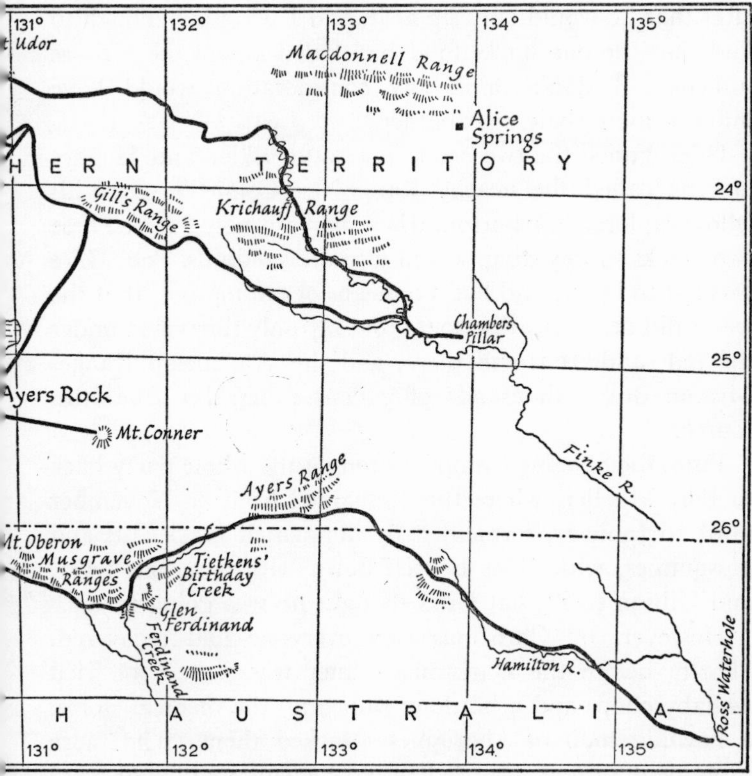

xpedition, 1873–4

was an exceedingly difficult operation to get water out of this abominable hole, as the bucket could not be dipped into it, nor could I reach the frightful fluid at all without hanging my head down, with my legs stretched across the mouth of it, while I baled the foetid mixture into the bucket with one of my boots, as I had no other utensil. What with the position I was in and the horrible odour which rose from the seething fluid, I was seized with violent retching. The horse gulped down the first half of the bucket with avidity, but after that he would only sip at it, and I was glad enough to find that the one bucketful I had baled out of the pit was sufficient. I don't think any consideration would have induced me to bale out another.'

Giles named the two creeks here after Elder and Hughes and he called the nearby Range the Colonel's, after his fellow explorer Warburton, whose name it now bears. These two creeks simply disappeared into the sandhills. Poor Giles was not to know, and had no means of finding out, that the water did not really disappear, but lay only thirty feet under the red sand. It is still there, and the Warburton Ranges Mission draws thousands of gallons every day from this source.

From the Shoeing Camp he brought the whole party back to Fort Mueller, where they remained from 20 November until 16 January, tormented by flies, small black ants and mosquitoes, with Giles himself down with a serious fever, and Gibson so ill that Giles thought he was going to die.

However, by Christmas Day everyone had recovered. Shortly before the Christmas dinner was served, of fried wallaby chops and a bottle of rum from the medical stores, a howling mob of Aborigines attacked them. 'The more prominent throng were led by an ancient individual who, having fitted a spear, was just in the act of throwing it down amongst us, when Gibson seized a rifle, and presented him with a conical Christmas box, which smote the rocks with such force, and in such near proximity to his hinder parts, that in a great measure it checked his fiery ardour, and induced most of his more timorous following to climb with most perturbed activity over the rocks.' A few more shots drove the rest away, and they settled down to 'an excellent dinner (for explorers)'. After dinner there was singing, first of all from Tietkens, with his fine, deep, clear voice. Then

Gibson delivered two or three love songs, not at all badly. Finally came Jimmy's turn. 'He said he didn't know no love songs, but he would give us Tommy or Paddy Brennan. This gentleman appears to have started in business as a highwayman in the romantic mountains of Limerick. One verse that Jimmy gave, and which pleased us most, because we couldn't quite understand it, was:

It was in sweet Limerick (er) citty
That he left his mother dear;
And in the Limerick (er) mountains,
He commenced his wild caroo-oo.

Upon our inquiring what a caroo was, Jimmy said he didn't know. No doubt it was something very desperate, and we considered we were perhaps upon a bit of a wild caroo ourselves.'

They stayed another three weeks making sorties to the north of up to 90 miles from this strange place, where earth-tremors shook rocks crashing down from the cliffs, and streams flowed at night and ceased in the day. Despite the name Giles had given it, of his beloved old scientist, he was not sorry to leave Fort Mueller, except for the garden he had planted and Gibson had indefatigably tended.

Seeds uncared-for, dropped in the wilderness, may not have come up, but here von Mueller would have rejoiced to see all the vegetables and the melons flourishing; of course, given a little regular water, Central Australian soil can grow almost anything.

Leaving Fort Mueller, 'really the most astonishing place it has ever been my fortune to visit', Giles perpetrated one of his finest specimens of rhyme-printed-as-prose. 'Though a most romantic region, its toils and dangers legion, my memory oft besieging, what time cannot restore; again I hear the shocks of the shattering of the rocks, see the wallabies in flocks, all trembling at the roar, or the volcanic reverberations, or seismatic detonations, which peculiar sensations I wish to know no more.'

Returning to prose, and borrowing the verse of more professional poets, amongst whom it seems a pity he did not include the Coleridge of *Kubla Khan*, Giles' spirits rose as he rode away. 'I had many strange, almost superstitious feelings with regard to this singular spot, for there was always a strange depression upon my spirits whilst here, arising partly perhaps from the constant dread of attacks from the hostile natives, and partly from the physical peculiarities of the region itself.

On all there hung a shadow and a fear,
A sense of mystery, the spirit daunted,
And said, as plain as whisper in the ear,
This region's haunted.

'On the 16th we departed, leaving to the native owners of the soil, this singular glen where the water flowed only in the night, where the earthquake and the dry thunderstorm occurred every day, and turned our backs for the last time upon

Their home by horror haunted,
Their desert land enchanted,

and plunged again into the northern wilderness.'

V

Death in the Desert

THE expedition left Fort Mueller late on 16 January, following the water points to the north surveyed by Giles and Tietkens until they reached the ranges, west of Lake Amadeus. Here, in the pools of a creek Giles called Sladen Water, an astonishing event happened. Gibson took a bath. Jimmy was so excited when he rushed to tell Giles that Giles immediately grabbed a rifle, thinking that natives were attacking. It was Gibson's first bath since Mt. Olga, eighteen weeks to a day. In fact they saw no natives in these ranges, and few animals or birds except a solitary eagle on the highest peak of a bare ridge, a 'solemn, solitary, and silent bird, like the Lorelei on her rock—above—beautifully, there'.

At their camps there was much repair work to do, as the packs and their clothes were torn to shreds after months of dragging through the bush. On another trip, Giles swore he would take leather packs, leather clothes and leather hearts. As it is, he writes, 'we keep continually patching our worst garments, hence our peculiar appearance, as our hats, shirts, and trousers, are here and there, so quilted with bits of old cloth, canvas, calico, basil, greenhide, and old blanket, that the original garment is scarcely anywhere visible. In the matter of boots the traveller must be able to shoe himself as well as his horses in these wild regions of the west. The explorer indeed should be possessed of a good few accomplishments—amongst these I may enumerate that he should be able to make a pie, shoe himself or his horse, jerk a doggerel verse or two, not for himself, but simply for the benefit or annoyance of others, and not necessarily for publication, nor as a guarantee of good faith; he must be able to take, and make, an observation now and again, mend a watch, kill or cure a horse as the times may require, make a pack-saddle, and understand something of astronomy, surveying, geography, geology, and mineralogy, et hoc, simile huic.'

The last week in January was spent exploring the Rawlinson Range; there was water at Fort McKellar, the Gorge of Tarns and a large semicircular basin, above which the lone eagle had sat, called the Circus.

On 1 February they set off for a mountain to the north-east, while the heat beat at them off the rocks and later from the great red sand hills, 108° in the shade, with no water and the horses 'excessively hollow'. Further out there was still no water, but Giles expected this to be remedied when they reached the mountain. But there was not a drop there. Suddenly, because of the horses, a fairly normal attempt to penetrate dry country turned into a desperate rush back to water and safety. The horses were rapidly failing. They all had names, and very individual characters, and were as much a part of the expedition as the men; and so was the dog, to which they gave the last drop of water they possessed.

Tietkens' riding horse, little Bluey, was the first to die. Giles then mounted Tietkens on Widge, 'a cool, calculating villain, that no ordinary work could kill, and he was lively as a cricket when Mr. Tietkens rode him away'. Giles then gives a series of extraordinarily vivid portraits of the other horses. 'Jimmy was mounted on a gray-hipped horse, which was also out on my former trip; he carried his rider well to the end. Gibson had mounted on a young bay mare, a creature as good as they make them; she was as merry and gay, as it is possible for any of her sex, even of the human kind, to be. Her proper name was the Fair Maid of Perth; but somehow, from her lively, troublesome, and wanton vagaries, they called her the Sow-Cow. My own riding-horse, a small, sleek, cunning little bay, in consequence of his persistent attention to his inwards, was called Guts. He would pull on his bridle all day long to eat, he would even pretend to eat spinifex; he was now very bad and footsore. Gibson and I overtook Mr. Tietkens and Jimmy, and we pushed on as fast as we could, the distance we had now to go, not being more than ten or eleven miles. The sandhills were exceedingly high and severe, but all the horses got over the last one.

'We were now in full view of the range, with the Gorge of Tarns not more than five miles away. But here Diamond and another, Pratt, that I had out by myself at the stinking pit in November, fell, never to rise. We took off their packs and left them on the ground. The thermometer then stood at 106° in the shade. We pushed on, intending to return immediately with water to the relief of these unfortunates. The pack-horses now presented a demoralized and disorganized rout, travelling in a long single file, for it was quite impossible to keep the tail up with the leaders. I shall try to give my reader some slight idea of them, if description is sufficiently palpable to do so. The real leader was an old black mare, blear-eyed from fly-wounds, for ever dropping tears of salt rheum, fat, large, strong, having carried her 180 lb. at starting, and now desperately thirsty and determined, knowing to an inch where the water was; on she went, reaching the stony slopes about two miles from the water. Next came a rather herring-gutted, lanky bay horse, which having been bought at the Peake, I called Peveril; he was generally poor, but always able, if not willing, for his work. Then came a big bay cob, and an old flea-bitten gray called Buggs, that got bogged in the Stemodia Viscosa Creek, and a nuggetty-black harness-horse called Darkie, always very fat. These last three carried 200 lb. each at starting. Then Banks, the best saddle-horse I have, and which I had worked too much in dry trips before reaching this range; he was very much out of sorts and footsore. Then an iron-grey colt, called Diaway, having been very poor and miserable when first purchased, but he was a splendid horse. Then came the sideways-going old crab, Terrible Billy. He was always getting into the most absurd predicaments—poor old creature; got down our throats at last!—falling into holes, and up and down slopes, going at them sideways, without the slightest confidence in himself, or apparent fear of consequences; but the old thing always did his work well enough. Blackie next, a handsome young colt with a white stripe down his face, and very fast; and Formby, a bay that had done excellent harness-work with Diamond on the road to the Peake; he was a great weight-carrier. The next was Hollow Back, who had once been a fine-paced and good jumping horse, but now only fit for packing; he was very well bred and very game. The next was Giant Despair, a perfect marvel. He was a chestnut, old, large-framed, gaunt, and bony, with screwed and lately staked feet. Life for him seemed but one unceasing round of toil, but he was made of iron; no distance and no weight was too much for him. He sauntered along after the leaders, looking not a whit the worse than when he left the last water, going neither faster nor slower than his wont. He was dreadfully destructive with his pack-bags, for he would never get out of the road for anything less than a gum-tree. Tommy and Badger, two of my former expedition horses; Tommy and Hippy I bought a second time from Carmichael, when coming up to the Peake. Tommy was poor, old, and footsore, the most wonderful horse for his size in harness I ever saw. Badger, his mate, was a big ambling cob, able to carry a ton, but the greatest slug of a horse I ever came across; he seems absolutely to require flogging as a tonic; he must be flogged out of camp, and flogged into it again, mile after mile, day after day, from water and to it. He was now, as usual, at the tail of the straggling mob, except Gibson's former riding-horse called Trew. He was an excellent little horse, but now so terribly footsore he could scarcely drag himself along; he was one of six best of the lot.'

Although Tietkens and Giles returned with water for the fallen horses, it was too late. They had lost four horses, Bluey, Diamond, Pratt and the cob. Giles 'called the vile mountain which had caused me this disaster, Mount Destruction'.

The prospects for the expedition were grim, whether they went forward into the desert, or back to Fort Mueller, 112 miles away. Giles decided to retreat to Sladen Water, where their rest was interrupted by one of the worst attacks from the natives that they had experienced. On this, as on other occasions, Giles gave the order to fire above and then below the natives, but in the last extremity, at them. He never says how many were killed or wounded.

On 20 February Giles and Jimmy Andrews set off towards the south-west. Although tortured by ants and heat, they at least had plenty of pigeons for food, as there had been at Sladen Water; they got enough for breakfast at one shot. When they broke clear of the ranges the country ahead looked frightful, and soon they were plunging up and down great red sandhills, until at the end of the third day they reached some low hills they had been aiming for. But there was no water there. The sun set red, huge and angry, and Giles watching it, full of wild and incongruous thoughts, wondered about his fellow-explorers, Warburton and Gosse; in fact, Warburton was that very day being feted in Perth, after his crossing to the Indian Ocean.

Giles did not know how he could get back; it was certainly impossible to go on. If only he had camels! The horses were dreadfully distressed. 'To see a horse in a state of great thirst is terrible, the natural cavity opens to an extraordinary size, and the creature strains and makes the most lamentable noises. Mares are generally worse in these cases than horses. Old Buggs and the mare were nearly dead. Diaway suffered less than the others. We had yet a small quantity of water in our bag, and it was absolutely necessary to sacrifice it to the horses if we wished them ever to return. We had but three pints, which we gave to Buggs and the mare, Diaway getting none.'

Fortunately they managed to stagger back to the gorge where there was water, and where Giles was again tortured by ants all through a sleepless night. When they got safely back to Sladen Water, Giles had not slept for a week.

The next fortnight went by in a survey of the country to the east as a possible line of retreat to save going back via Fort Mueller on already travelled tracks, although Giles was still determined to continue to the west when cooler weather came. Giles discovered and named the Petermann Range, and Tietkens and he had a very unpleasant brush with the natives; in fighting them off the horses seemed to scare them as much as anything else. On this journey Giles went within sixty miles of his favourite natural wonder, Mt. Olga. In his diary, desperate for even wilder similes than before, he rapidly likened it to five or six enormous pink hay-stacks; several monstrous kneeling pink elephants; and its highest point to a gigantic pink dumper, or Chinese gong viewed sideways. Perhaps he had been raiding the medicinal room again.

Back at the main camp, food was running very short, with no meat and little flour left; also ammunition was low, especially as Jimmy and Gibson were always loosing off fusillades at ducks or pigeons without hitting any. So they built a smoke house, and sadly put a Snider bullet into Terrible Billy and sliced him up, and smoked him; 'a column of smoke ascends from the immolated Billy night and day.' The job was finished on 3 April. On 7 April they left camp and established a new depot to the west at Fort McKellar near the Gorge of Tarns. From here Giles intended to make one last attempt 'to grapple with that western desert'. It was a pleasant change that before they left they had a very friendly meeting with a number of Aborigines.

On 19 April Giles announced that he had made up his mind 'to try what impression a hundred miles would make on the country to the west'. Gibson immediately volunteered to go with him, saying he had been left behind too often. Giles would much rather have taken Tietkens, but gave in, and set off the next day with Gibson. Giles was riding the Fair Maid of Perth, Gibson the big ambling horse Badger, and they packed the big cob with a pair of waterbags holding 20 gallons, and Darkie with two five-gallon kegs of water, and the food and bedding.

They watered that night at the Circus creek, and the next day, the 21st, continued to the west. Giles, always interested in his fellow explorers, and generous about them, remarked that it was the anniversary of Burke and Wills' return to the depot at Cooper's Creek. Gibson had never heard of Burke and Wills, so Giles told him the story, casually mentioning that Wills had a brother who had lost his life in Polar exploration with Sir John Franklin. 'Gibson then said, "Oh! I had a brother who died with Franklin at the North Pole, and my father had a deal of trouble to get his pay from Government." He seemed in a very jocular vein this morning, which was not often the case, for he was usually rather sulky, sometimes for days together, and he said, "How is it, that in all these exploring expeditions a lot of people go and die?" I said, "I don't know, Gibson, how it is, but there are many dangers in exploring, besides accidents and attacks from the natives, that may at any time cause the death of some of the people engaged in it; but I believe want of judgment, or knowledge, or courage in individuals, often brought about their deaths. Death, however, is a thing that must occur to every one sooner or later." To this he replied, "Well, I shouldn't like to die in this part of the country, anyhow." In this sentiment I quite agreed with him, and the subject dropped.'

Ominously, when they stopped for an hour to turn the horses out and have a meal, Giles found that Gibson had not packed the bag full of smoked horse meat as ordered; instead of there being enough for two for a week, there was scarcely enough for one. However, a compensation was that the going was relatively easy as the parallel sand hills were running east and west. Sixty miles out, the sandhills ceased and they were on flat ground covered with fine gravel. One of the big waterbags had been leaking, so Giles decided to turn the two pack horses loose to find their way back to the Circus; against Giles' advice, Gibson insisted on swapping his Badger for the big cob. Here they hung the five-gallon kegs and the pack saddles in a tree, after which the place was always known as the Kegs.

On the 23rd they were still on the endless undulations of the plain, covered with spinifex and with occasional patches of mulga or mallee. Ninety miles out from the Circus Giles saw a line of low stony ridges about 10 miles off. He decided to push on to these, but Gibson saw others closer, and they made for these, as his cob was knocking up. From a stony hill eight miles farther on Giles could see distant hills, 25–30 miles away, which he longed to reach, and later named the Alfred and Marie Range.

But he was not to know whether they held water, as Gibson said his horse would never reach them. In fact there is very often water in these ridges, and for months after rain water lies in long pools along ravines which run north into the desert. They turned back, and had gone only a mile when the cob lay down and refused to move. There was nothing to do but leave him to die, and carry on, taking it in turns to ride the Fair Maid of Perth.

When they had got back to about thirty miles from the Kegs, Giles called a halt. They shared their last pint of water and then Giles said, ' "Look here, Gibson, you see we are in a most terrible fix with only one horse, therefore only one can ride, and one must remain behind. I shall remain: and now listen to me. If the mare does not get water soon she will die; therefore ride right on; get to the Kegs, if possible, to-night, and give her water. Now the cob is dead there'll be all the more for her; let her rest for an hour or two, and then get over a few more miles by morning, so that early to-morrow you will sight the Rawlinson, at twenty-five miles from the Kegs. Stick to the tracks, and never leave them. Leave as much water in one keg for me as you can afford after watering the mare and filling up your own bags, and, remember, I depend upon you to bring me relief. Rouse Mr. Tietkens, get fresh horses and more water-bags, and return as soon as you possibly can. I shall of course endeavour to get down the tracks also."

'He then said if he had a compass he thought he could go better at night. I knew he didn't understand anything about compasses, as I had often tried to explain them to him. The one I had was a Gregory's Patent, of a totally different construction from ordinary instruments of the kind, and I was very loth to part with it, as it was the only one I had. However, he was so anxious for it that I gave it him, and he departed. I sent one final shout after him to stick to the tracks, to which he replied, "All right," and the mare carried him out of sight almost immediately. That was the last ever seen of Gibson.'

Giles had thirty miles to go to reach the Kegs. The afternoon was very hot, and he did not think he could arrive before the next evening, if at all. He followed the tracks after dark by the moon, but when that went down he was forced to halt; he was too choked by thirst to sleep. At first light he was on the move again, and he reached the Kegs at midday on 24 April 1874. Gibson had been there, and watered the mare, and left Giles a little over two gallons of water. In his agony of thirst he could have drunk the lot, but he rationed himself severely, not knowing how many days would pass before help would come; it could not be less than five days. When his throat was moist again he realized he was ravenously hungry. All the food he could find in the bags was 'eleven sticks of dirty, sandy, smoked horse, averaging about an ounce and a half each, at the bottom of a pack bag'. He had no water to spare to boil them, so he devoured a couple of sticks raw.

Sitting in the meagre shade of the tree, Giles reflected on his desperate situation. If he waited for help, he would probably be dead before it came. If he went on, he would have to carry the keg, which with the water weighed 35 lb. He had to have a blanket for his shoulder when carrying the keg, and with his revolver and cartridge pouch, knife and other oddments, he would be carrying a load of about 50 lb.

The only hope was to stand up and go on. Under the weight he could scarcely move. By next morning, travelling by moonlight as far as possible, he had covered only three miles, and in the days and nights that flowed over him he could manage only about five miles a day.

'To people who cannot comprehend such a region it may seem absurd that a man could not travel faster than that. All I can say is, there may be men who could do so, but most men in the position I was in would simply have died of hunger and thirst, for by the third or fourth day—I couldn't tell which—my horse meat was all gone, I had to remain in what scanty shade I could find during the day, and I could only travel by night.

'When I lay down in the shade in the morning I lost all consciousness, and when I recovered my senses I could not tell whether one day or two or three had passed. At one place I am sure I must have remained over forty-eight hours. At a certain place on the road—that is to say, on the horse tracks—at about fifteen miles from the Kegs—at twenty-five miles the Rawlinson could again be sighted—I saw that the tracks of the two loose horses we had turned back from there had left the main line of tracks, which ran east and west, and had turned about east-south-east, and the tracks of the Fair Maid of Perth, I was grieved to see, had gone on them also. I felt sure Gibson would soon find his error, and return to the main line. I was unable to investigate this any farther in my present position. I followed them about a mile, and then returned to the proper line, anxiously looking at every step to see if Gibson's horse tracks returned into them.

'They never did, nor did the loose horse tracks either. Generally speaking, whenever I saw a shady desert oak-tree there was an enormous bull-dog ants' nest under it, and I was prevented from sitting in its shade. On what I thought was the 27th I almost gave up the thought of walking any farther, for the exertion in this dreadful region, where the triodia was almost as high as myself, and as thick as it could grow, was quite overpowering, and being starved, I felt quite light-headed. After sitting down, on every occasion when I tried to get up again, my head would swim round, and I would fall down oblivious for some time. Being in a chronic state of burning thirst, my general plight was dreadful in the extreme. A bare and level sandy waste would have been Paradise to walk over compared to this. My arms, legs, thighs, both before and behind, were so punctured with spines, it was agony only to exist; the slightest movement and in went more spines, where they broke off in the clothes and flesh, causing the whole of the body that was punctured to gather into minute pustules, which were continually growing and bursting. My clothes, especially inside my trousers, were a perfect mass of prickly points.

'My great hope and consolation now was that I might soon meet the relief party. But where was the relief party? Echo could only answer—where? About the 29th I had emptied the keg, and was still over twenty miles from the Circus. Ah! who can imagine what twenty miles means in such a case? But in this April's ivory moonlight I plodded on, desolate indeed, but all undaunted, on this lone, unhallowed shore. At last I reached the Circus, just at the dawn of day. Oh, how I drank! how I reeled! how hungry I was! how thankful I was that I had so far at least escaped from the jaws of that howling wilderness, for I was once more upon the range, though still twenty miles from home.

'There was no sign of the tracks, of any one having been here since I left it. The water was all but gone. The solitary eagle still was there. I wondered what could have become of Gibson; he certainly had never come here, and how could he reach the fort without doing so?'

Giles stayed at the Circus, drinking and drinking, until about 10 a.m. the next day, and then crawled away towards the Gorge of Tarns. 'Just as I got clear of the bank of the creek, I heard a faint squeak, and looking about I saw, and immediately caught, a small dying wallaby, whose marsupial mother had evidently thrown it from her pouch. It only weighed about two ounces, and was scarcely furnished yet with fur. The instant I saw it, like an eagle I pounced upon it and ate it, living, raw, dying—fur, skin, bones, skull, and all. The delicious taste of that creature I shall never forget.'

Late that night he had only managed eleven miles, and lay down, choking for water. While lying down he thought he heard the sounds of a galloping horse, and he vaguely thought it might be Gibson on the Fair Maid, but they disappeared in the direction of the camp.

At one o'clock in the morning of 1 May he reached the Gorge of Tarns. Although there was the blessed relief of water again, he was almost too exhausted to go on. But he did, and by daylight was waking Tietkens, 'who stared at me as though I had been one, new risen from the dead'. Neither Gibson nor the horses had returned. 'I was the only one of six living creatures—two men and four horses—that had returned, or were now ever likely to return, from that desert.'

Tietkens had been extremely anxious about their safety, and had only just come back from leaving some meat and supplies at the Circus. His horse had made the noise Giles had heard during the night.

Tietkens and Giles were horrified at what must now be the certainty of Gibson's loss. Not so Jimmy. 'When we woke Jimmy up he was delighted to see me, but when told about Gibson, he said something about he knowed he worn't no good in the bush, but as long as I had returned, &c., &c.'

Giles was prostrate with exhaustion, but determined to go back into the desert and look for Gibson, or at least for his remains. (And no doubt, after the comedy of their parting, for that Gregory's Patent compass. Also, Giles ruefully records, Gibson had his field glasses.)

Any normal man would need a week to get over what Giles had just gone through. But a day later Giles was being helped onto his horse Blackie, and was setting off with Tietkens on Diaway, and Widge, Formby and Hippy carrying packs. They found Gibson's tracks on the Fair Maid, and followed them until they were four nights away from water, but it was very slow work, as the wind and the sand and the lizards had often covered the tracks, and also Gibson had foolishly turned and carried on at right angles to the terrible parallel sandhills. Giles realized that if he and Tietkens did not turn back they also would lose their lives; indeed, the return journey was very hard on both men and horses, and by the time they reached the Depot, Giles was almost more exhausted than when he had walked in alone.

'I called this terrible region that lies between the Rawlinson Range and the next permanent water that may eventually be found to the west, Gibson's Desert, after this first white victim to its horrors.'

When, ninety years later, Len Beadell and his team of Land-Rovers, bulldozer, grader and trucks was coping with the appalling difficulties of putting a road through this area, Beadell nearly lost his life reconnoitring Gibson's Desert in the Land-Rover. Beadell is not given to Giles' baroque superlatives of language, but 'dreadful', 'nightmare', 'desperation', are the words he uses about this country. Beadell considers that Giles was being too self-sacrificing in giving Gibson the horse, and walking himself. But Gibson would almost certainly have died before Giles could have returned.

Despite Giles' utter exhaustion, he was determined to try once more to find Gibson's remains; 'I could not endure the thought of leaving Gibson's last resting-place unknown.' But all the water at the Circus was now gone, and the only hope was to use as base another rock-hole which Tietkens and Gibson had found; however, it proved useless.

When he and Tietkens returned to Fort McKellar they found Jimmy overjoyed to see them, as he had heroically (at least, according to Jimmy) fought off a prodigious onslaught of savages. Jimmy was no great ornament to the white race, but Giles obviously thought him worth a couple of dozen Aborigines. 'If he had killed ten per cent. for all the cartridges he fired away, I should think he would have destroyed the whole tribe; but he appeared to have been too flurried to have hit many of them. They threw several spears and great quantities of stones down from the rocks; it was fortunate he had a palisade to get inside of. Towards night he seems to have driven them off, and he and the little dog watched all night. It must indeed have been something terrible that would keep Jimmy awake all night. Before daylight on Sunday the natives came to attack him again; he had probably improved in his aim by his previous day's practice, for at length he was able to drive them away screeching and yelling, the wounded being carried in the arms of the others. One fellow, Jimmy said, came rushing up to give him his quietus, and began dancing about the camp and pulling over all the things, when Jimmy suddenly caught up a shot gun loaded with heavy long-shot cartridges, of which I had about a dozen left for defence, and before the fellow could get away, he received the full charge in his body. Jimmy said he bounded up in the air, held up his arms, shrieked, and screamed, but finally ran off with all the others, and they had not troubled him since. I gave the lad great praise for his action. He had had a most fortunate escape from most probably a cruel death, if indeed these animals would not have actually eaten him.'

By this time the last shreds of Terrible Billy had been consumed, and it was time to hang up another horse in the newly completed smoke-house. This time it was Tommy, a Victorian, very old and very poor, scarcely a drop of oil in his dry bones. While he smoked, they made preparations to depart. The desert had beaten Giles this time, and also the loss of a man, and so many horses. 'Had Gibson not been lost I should certainly have pushed out west again and again. To say I was sorry to abandon such a work in such a region, though true, may seem absurd, but it must be remembered I was pitted, or had pitted myself, against Nature, and a second time I was conquered. The expedition had failed in its attempt to reach the west, but still it had done something. It would at all events leave a record. Our stores and clothes were gone, we had nothing but horseflesh to eat, and it is scarcely to be wondered at if neither Mr. Tietkens nor Jimmy could receive my intimation of my intention to retreat otherwise than with pleasure, though both were anxious, as I was, that our efforts should be successful. In our present circumstances, however, nothing more could be done.'

On 21 May they began their retreat from Fort McKellar. The weather was delightful, the country beautiful, the going easy; everyone's spirits should have been high. Giles was moved to quote Bunyan instead of Byron. 'It is impossible that I should ever forget Sladen Water or the Pass of the Abencerrages: "Methinks I am as well in this valley as I have been anywhere else in all our journey; the place methinks suits with my spirit. I love to be in such places, where there is no rattling with coaches, nor rumbling with wheels. Methinks here one may, without much molestation, be thinking what he is, and whence he came; what he has done, and to what the king has called him." ' But despite everything, 'a gloom covered our retreat, and we travelled along almost in silence'.

The natives continued to shadow them, and as usual were suspected of harm even when they did nothing. Merely to be in rifle-range was enough. However, even here something emerges of the humorous side of Giles, the comedy of the incongruity of the white man in the bush, a human comedy that would have appealed to his hero Byron, and which also went with a Byronic capacity for exaltation and melancholy. Childe Harold and Don Juan are two sides of the one complex character. 'One aboriginal fiend, of the Homo sapiens genus, while we were sitting down sewing bags as usual, sneaked so close upon us, down the rocks behind the camp, that he could easily have touched or tomahawked—if he had one—either of us, before he was discovered. My little dog was sometimes too lazy to obey, when a little distance off, the command to sit, or stand up; in that case I used to send him a telegram, as I called it—

that is to say, throw a little stone at him, and up he would sit immediately. This sneak of a native was having a fine game with us. Cocky was lying down near Mr. Tietkens, when a stone came quietly and roused him, causing him to sit up. Mr. Tietkens patted him, and he lay down again. Immediately after another stone came, and up sat Cocky. This aroused Mr. Tietkens' curiosity, as he didn't hear me speak to the dog, and he said, "Did you send Cocky a telegram?" I said, "No." "Well then," said he, "somebody did twice: did you, Jimmy?" "No." "Oh!" I exclaimed, "it's those blacks!" We jumped up and looked at the low rocks behind us, where we saw about half-a-dozen sidling slowly away behind them. Jimmy ran on top, but they had all mysteriously disappeared. We kept a sharp look out after this, and fired a rifle off two or three times, when we heard some groans and yells in front of us up the creek gorge.'

Following along the Rawlinson and Petermann Ranges, by 5 June they reached their old favourite Mt. Olga, and camped against the south face, with the luxury of running water beside them. In his narrative Giles rather quaintly remarks, apparently unaware that he is confusing himself with the Almighty, 'Could I be buried at Mount Olga, I should certainly borrow Sir Christopher Wren's epitaph, Circumspice si monumentum requiris.'

On the 9th they moved to Ayers Rock, twenty miles away, and camped in a cave, 'ornamented in the usual aboriginal fashion'. Giles would no doubt have been staggered to know that ninety years later the anthropologist C. P. Mountford would write a whole book about the aboriginal legends connected with this most sacred rock. However, if he was blind to primitive religion, Giles had the most acute eye for the physical appearance of this 'mammoth monolith'. No one has made a better comparison of the entirely different characters of those two extraordinary outcrops of rock. 'The great difference between it (Ayers Rock) and Mount Olga is in the rock formation, for this is one solid granite stone, and is part and parcel of the original rock, which, having been formed after its state of fusion in the beginning, has there remained, while the aged Mount Olga has been thrown up subsequently from below. Mount Olga is the more wonderful and grotesque; Mount Ayers the more ancient and sublime.'

Before they left the Rock, they built another smoke-house and killed old Hollow Back and smoked him. For anyone wishing to smoke a horse, Giles' instructions could not be bettered. 'The smoke-house is formed of four main stakes stuck into the ground and coming nearly together at the top, with cross sticks all the way down, and covered over with tarpaulins, so that no smoke can escape except through the top. The meat is cut into thin strips, and becomes perfectly permeated with smoke. So soon as all was ready, down went poor Hollow Back. He was in what is called good working condition, but he had not a vestige of fat about him. The only adipose matter we could obtain from him was by boiling his bones, and the small quantity of oil thus obtained would only fry a few meals of steaks. When that was done we had to fry or parboil them in water. Our favourite method of cooking the horseflesh after the fresh meat was eaten, was by first boiling and then pounding with the axe, tomahawk head, and shoeing hammer, then cutting it into small pieces, wetting the mass, and binding it with a pannikin of flour, putting it into the coals in the frying-pan, and covering the whole with hot ashes. But the flour would not last, and those delicious horse-dampers, though now but things of the past, were by no means relegated to the limbo of forgotten things. The boiled-up bones, hoofs, shanks, skull, &c., of each horse, though they failed to produce a sufficient quantity of oil to please us, yet in the cool of the night resolved themselves into a consistent jelly that stank like rotten glue, and at breakfast at least, when this disgusting stuff was in a measure coagulated, we would request one another with the greatest politeness to pass the gluepot. Had it not been that I was an inventor of transcendent genius, even this last luxury would have been debarred us. We had been absent from civilization, so long, that our tin billies, the only boiling utensils we had, got completely worn or burnt out at the bottoms, and as the boilings for glue and oil must still go on, what were we to do with billies with no bottoms? Although as an inventor I can allow no one to depreciate my genius, I will admit there was but one thing that could be done, and those muffs Tietkens and Jimmy actually advised me to do what I had invented, which was simply—all great inventions are simple—to cover the bottoms with canvas, and embed the billies half-way up their sides in cold ashes, and boil from the top instead of the bottom, which of course we did, and these were our glue- and flesh-pots. The tongue, brains, kidneys, and other tit-bits of course were eaten first.'

On 23 June they left Ayers Rock, after a very friendly meeting with some natives, who were 'rather good, though extremely wild-looking young men. One of them had splendid long black curls waving in the wind, hanging down nearly to his middle; the other two had chignons.' They relished the smoked horse which Giles gave them.

Giles led his party north-east, crossing the arm of Lake Amadeus 'on a broad streak of bushes and boughs laid down by Mr. Gosse', and then making for Gill's Range, with an easy journey down to the Finke River following the tracks of his own 1872 expedition.

On 10 July they were at the Telegraph Line, and met the first white man they had seen for nearly a year, a contractor called Frost taking his teams north up the Line with supplies for the Telegraph Stations. This good man immediately gave orders for his horses to be unyoked, poured off a quart of rum from his hogshead, boiled billies for tea, and gave them food; some splendid fat corned beef, 'and mustard, and well-cooked damper were put before us, and oh, didn't we eat! Then pots of jams and tins of butter were put on our plates whole, and were scooped up with spoons, till human organisms could do no more. We were actually full—full to repletion. Then we had some grog. Next we had a sleep, and then at sundown another exquisite meal. It made our new friends shudder to look at our remaining stock of Hollow Back, when we emptied it out on a tarpaulin and told them that was what we had been living on. However, I made them a present of it for their dogs. Most of the teamsters knew Gibson, and expressed their sorrow at his mishap; some of them also knew he was married.' Giles sold them some firearms and some horses and gear; not as many horses as Frost wanted, but Giles would not part with Guts, Widge and a couple more.

On 13 July, Giles reached Charlotte Waters and was given a splendid welcome by his namesake, young Christopher Giles, and then all down the Line old friends looked after the gaunt travellers whom many people had thought to have perished in the desert. Then from Blinman down to Adelaide there were the almost forgotten comforts of a mail-coach and a train.

Giles' expedition to cross the continent from the Telegraph Line to the Indian Ocean had been a failure. In Adelaide he learned that another expedition was in the field, travelling from west to east under John Forrest.

Actually at this very time Forrest was at Blyth Creek, and just about to make his final conquering dash across Gibson's Desert to Giles' Warburton Range. When Giles was in Melbourne, reporting back to his patron, Baron von Mueller, he heard that Forrest had safely reached the Telegraph Line.

For his achievements, Forrest was given 5,000 acres of land by the Government. Giles received nothing, though his sense of ironic humour relished the 'many compliments from men of standing'. 'The truest, perhaps, was from a gentleman who patted me on the back and said, "Ah, Ernest, my boy, you should never have come back; you should have sent your journal home by Tietkens and died out there yourself." ' To keep body and soul together, he was given a temporary appointment by Graham Berry, Premier of Victoria (for two months) at that time, and he busied himself getting his journal and map in order, to be presented to the South Australian government as required under the terms of their niggardly support.

Giles had had a hard time. As he said, 'we passed through a baptism worse indeed than that of fire—the baptism of no water'. In the most extraordinary activity in the history of Australian exploration, there had, almost simultaneously, been four expeditions in the field, all attempting the crossing from South to West Australia, or vice versa. Edward John Eyre had made the first crossing of all, in his incredible journey around the edge of the Nullarbor and on to King George Sound in 1840–1. From the centre of the continent, Warburton had succeeded (only just) in crossing to the West with camels in 1873–4. Gosse, with camels, failed in 1873. Forrest, with horses, succeeded in 1874. Had Gibson not perished, Giles might have met Forrest somewhere west of the desert that would have had another name.

Giles had too generous a character to be jealous of his fellow explorers, and he was too fine a bushman not to know the luck of the game. He had his eye on another expedition, with camels. Soon after his return to civilization, von Mueller introduced him to Thomas Elder, Australia's only camel-owner. Elder and Giles immediately began to draw up plans for a new expedition, which would cross from east to west through unexplored country below the 29th parallel of latitude. Undeterred by thirst, sand and spinifex, Giles was off again. One wonders if he paused to consider whether smoked camel would taste better or worse than smoked horse.

VI

The Third Expedition—Camels and Horses

Before Giles was to leave on his new expedition for Perth, Thomas Elder asked him to survey some pastoral country near Fowler's Bay, for a would-be squatter in England. This he did, and he casually adds that he 'visited the remote locality of Eucla Harbour' on the boundary of Western and South Australia. With horses this was a strenuous trip in itself, although following the Telegraph Line; it was only 34 years since Eyre had first travelled between the waterless Nullarbor Plain and the sudden edge of the stupendous cliffs that guard the Great Australian Bight.

Giles now had to cut across country to Elder's camel depot at Beltana station, 300 miles north of Adelaide. This was only 375 miles as the crow flies from Fowler's Bay, but owing to salt lakes and other obstructions Giles had to travel nearly 700 miles to reach it, much of this through hard, dense mallee scrub, and spinifex sandhills.

His plan was to go north to a native waterhole called Youldeh, the modern Ooldea, which he could use as a depot on his later journey west, and then strike east for the northern end of Lake Torrens. He left on 13 March 1875 with four white men, including the police trooper from Fowler's Bay, four blacks, horses and two camels and a calf.

They had a hot trip to Youldeh, which was even hotter, lying at the bottom of a funnel-like hollow in the red sandhills, concentrating the heat on the sandy soak which they had to dig out and slab up to make into a proper well. Fortunately the supply of water was good. It was the first time Giles had been out with camels, and he was very impressed with the way in which they calmly stood in the shade of a mulga tree eating the foliage around their heads, while the hobbled horses went snorting and plunging over the sandhills, terrified of the scent and presence of these strange beasts.

The old Aborigine with them, Jimmy, was the first of his race with whom Giles reached close and friendly terms. He 'looked like a thoroughbred', was proud and honourable, and altogether 'was a very agreeable old gentleman'. Jimmy had a hearty dislike for the country to the north across the red sandhills, and its wild aboriginal inhabitants, the Cockata, who were given to raiding the Fowler's Bay natives. When some horses got loose, the younger Aborigines would not go north to look for them, and Mr. Richards, the trooper, who was returning to Fowler's Bay, never saw his horse again.

Giles consulted with Jimmy about the country to the east, and Jimmy drew a sand-map and rattled off the names of five waterholes, the furthest, Wynbring, being about six sleeps away; 'this, according to our rendering, as Jimmy declared also that it was mucka close up, only long way, we considered to be about 120 miles.' This was Jimmy's mother's country and he had not visited it since he was a boy; however, he had no qualms about leading them into it, at least as far as Wynbring, for to Jimmy that was the end of the world.

Giles decided to travel light, so sent everyone back to Fowler's Bay except Peter Nicholls the cook and old Jimmy; he took three horses and the camels, and had a hard job making a pack saddle for the bull. The horses were still very frightened of the camels, and indeed the human beings were none too sure what to expect, never having managed them before. Nicholls rode the cow, not with great success. 'The old cow that he was riding would scarcely budge for him at all. If he beat her she would lie down, yell, squall, spit, and roll over on her saddle, and behave in such a manner that, neither of us knowing anything about camels, we thought she was going to die. The sandhills were oppressively steep, and the old wretch perspired to such a degree, and altogether became such an unmanageable nuisance, that I began to think camels could not be half the wonderful animals I had fondly imagined.

'The bull, Mustara, behaved much better. He was a most affectionate creature, and would kiss people all day long; but the Lord help any one who would try to kiss the old cow, for she would cover them all over with—well, we will call it spittle, but it is worse than that. The calf would kiss also when caught, but did not care to be caught too often.'

The going was rough, and some of Jimmy's waterholes yielded only a stinking black fluid which the horses drank but the human beings left alone. One waterhole, Pylebung, astonished Giles by being built up into a dam by the natives, 'the first piece of work of art or usefulness that I had ever seen in all my travels in Australia'. It was surrounded by one of those lovely grassy plains, over whose pale expanses the silver grey foliage of mulga and myall sweeps down, that suddenly open out (like a gentleman's park) in the mallee wastes of untouched Australia. Giles found a path, and heaps of stones at the foot of each long-haired casuarina tree, and immediately 'felt sure that it was one of those places where the men of this region perform inhuman mutilations upon the youths and maidens of their tribe'. Despite his fondness for Jimmy, Giles could not trust any Aborigine not to commit some hideous desecration of the chastity of Nature; when questioned, Jimmy denied that he had ever officiated at such doings.

Old Jimmy did always lead them to water, but not in a straight line. 'Sometimes when leading us through the scrubs, and having travelled for some miles nearly east, he would notice a tree or a sandhill, or something that he remembered, and would turn suddenly from that point in an entirely different direction, towards some high and severe sandhill; here he would climb a tree. After a few minutes' gazing about, he would descend, mount his horse, and go off on some new line, and in the course of a mile or so he would stop at a tree, and tell us that when a little boy he got a 'possum out of a hole which existed in it. At another place he said his mother was bitten by a wild dog, which she was digging out of a hole in the ground; and thus we came to Wynbring at last.' Wynbring was not a mountain, as described by old Jimmy, but a bare expanse of granite perhaps fifty feet high and an acre or two in extent, standing alone in the midst of an open plain in the scrubby country. Yet it held an ample supply of good water.

Until this expedition, Giles' contact with Aborigines had always been tangential. They appeared behind rocks or over sandhills, sometimes friendly, sometimes wailing and waving spears. To Giles they were all simply savages, devoid of intellectual or artistic capacity, a prey to gross superstitions. Although he walked and rode for thousands of miles over their native grounds, he did not understand the irony of the ecology of the country he was exploring, that to the naked savages it was home, but unrelentingly hostile to the clothed explorer, even one accustomed to

Byron for breakfast. Giles' sensitivity to the spirit of place, his genuine spiritual exaltation before these simplicities of red rock and sand, grey mulga and deep blue sky, did not extend to the intimate communion already established between Australia and its aboriginal inhabitants. That is, until he travelled with old Jimmy, the safety of his expedition depending on Jimmy's recognition of some tiny detail in the immense apparent uniformity of the scrub and landscape. No one who has not travelled in these arid regions can realize the subtleties that hide in their immense distances. Old Jimmy could recite them like poetry learned in childhood.

Giles was 'struck with admiration' that old Jimmy had safely led them to Wynbring. 'How he or any other human being, not having the advantages of science at his command to teach him, by the use of the heavenly bodies, how to find the position of any locality, could possibly return to the places he had visited in such a wilderness, especially as it was done by the recollection of spots which, to a white man, have no special features and no guiding points, was really marvellous. We had travelled at least 120 miles eastward from Youldeh, and when there, this old fellow had told us that he had not visited any of the places he was going to take me to since his boyhood; this at the very least must have been forty years ago, for he was certainly fifty, if not seventy years old. The knowledge possessed by these children of the desert is preserved owing to the fact that their imaginations are untrammelled, the denizens of the wilderness, having their mental faculties put to but few uses, and all are concentrated on the object of obtaining food for themselves and their offspring. Whatever ideas they possess, and they are by no means dull or backward in learning new ones, are ever keen and young, and Nature has endowed them with an undying mental youth, until their career on earth is ended. As says a poet, speaking of savages or men in a state of nature—

There the passions may revel unfettered,
And the heart never speak but in truth;
And the intellect, wholly unlettered,
Be bright with the freedom of youth.

'Assuredly man in a savage state, is by no means the unhappiest of mortals.'

He had certainly made Giles happy for a while, for Wynbring supplied the party with the 'three requisites that constitute an explorer's happiness—that is to say, wood, water, and grass'.

Old Jimmy not only brought Giles into contact with the bonds of instinct and knowledge connecting the Aborigine and the land; he actually brought him into physical contact with his dark race. There were many signs of native life around Wynbring, and old Jimmy went off with a gun (Giles had taken the precaution of unloading it) to round up some blacks and bring them to the white man's camp.

'Away he went, and returned with five captives, an antiquated one-eyed old gentleman, with his three wives, and one baby belonging to the second wife, who had been a woman of considerable beauty. She was now rather past her prime. What the oldest wife could ever have been like, it was impossible to guess, as now she seemed more like an old she-monkey than anything else. The youngest was in the first flush of youth and grace. The new old man was very tall, and had been very big and powerful, but he was now shrunken and grey with age. He ordered his wives to sit down in the shade of a bush near our camp; this they did. I walked towards the old man, when he immediately threw his aged arms round me, and clasped me rapturously to his ebony breast. Then his most ancient wife followed his example, clasping me in the same manner. The second wife was rather incommoded in her embrace by the baby in her arms, and it squalled horridly the nearer its mother put it to me. The third and youngest wife, who was really very pretty, appeared enchantingly bashful, but what was her bashfulness compared to mine, when compelled for mere form's sake to enfold in my arms a beautiful and naked young woman? It was really a distressing ordeal. She showed her appreciation of our company by the glances of her black and flashing eyes, and the exposure of two rows of beautifully even and pearly teeth.' These natives were all anxious to have white man's names, so Giles called 'the young beauty' Polly, and her husband Wynbring Tommy, the mother Mary, the baby Kitty and the oldest woman Judy.

There were diversions and beauties at Wynbring, but the heat was ferocious, always in the day around the 105° mark in the shade, and at night dropping only to the 80's. In addition humans and animals were tortured by flies, not only the ordinary little ones, but the big stinging March-flies that come persistently in to bite any area of exposed skin and raise an itchy, red lump.

The 1st of April was the hottest day Giles had ever known, and he resolved to move on, finding life almost insupportable. Old Jimmy knew nothing of the country ahead; he had reached his Ultima Thule. There was a mountain to the south-east which Giles called Mt. Finke, and although the old local native said there was no water there, Giles decided to make a detour in that direction, as otherwise the only water he knew of was at Elder's cattle station, Finniss Springs, 250 miles away.

They set off again, the camels loaded with 50 gallons of water, watched over by old Jimmy who was leading no more. Giles rode ahead on his Chester, a fine chestnut cob, while Nicholls followed on Formby, a veteran of the last expedition. The going was terrible, up and down steep sandhills that trapped the heat, and the night was misery and unrest, with the horses and camels stirring. Giles should have listened to the old native, Wynbring Tommy, for Mt. Finke, when after 45 miles they reached it, 'was the most desolate heap on the face of the earth, having no water or places that could hold it'. They steered away for some ridges Giles had seen from its 1,000 ft. summit, but heat, thirst and the fearful country of alternate sand and scrub were too much for the horse old Jimmy was riding. They had to leave him lying on the sand, his saddle hung in the fork of a sandalwood tree. Ominously, he reminded Giles of Badger and Darkie in Gibson's Desert.

Rapidly the situation was deteriorating into one of the most dangerous Giles had ever been in. There was no water in the ridges, any more than there was in the dry clay pans where the camels had wandered looking for a drink. Giles' respect for the camels was increasing as the horses became weaker and weaker from heat and lack of water. 'They had received no water themselves, though they had laboured over the hideous sandhills, laden with the priceless fluid for the benefit of the horses, and it was quite evident the latter could not much longer live, in such a desert, whilst the former were now far more docile and obedient to us than when we started. Whenever the horses were given any water, we had to tie the camels up at some distance. The expression in these animals' eyes when they saw the horses drinking was extraordinary; they seemed as though they were going to speak, and had they done so, I know well they would have said, "You give those useless little pigmies the water that cannot save them, and you deny it to us, who have carried it, and will yet be your only saviours in the end." '

They were now 120 miles from the water at Wynbring, and Giles was again at the fatal crux. Should he risk lives by going on? Or, equally, should he risk them by attempting to go back over country so terrible that it had already killed one of the horses and reduced the whole party to exhaustion? Whichever decision Giles might make, old Jimmy was appalled at the white man's temerity, to go charging off into the wilderness without knowing the whereabout of the next waterhole.

For Giles, obviously the only solution was to go on. But 30 miles further into scrub as bad and dense as any they had seen, poor Chester, that Giles had now been leading for many miles, rolled on the ground in his death agony. Giles put him out of his misery with a bullet in his forehead.

By that night they were 168 miles from Wynbring, their water was almost gone, and there was only one horse, Formby, still alive. In the morning the horse was standing by the fire, vacantly watching it, and suddenly he seemed to think the flames were water and put his mouth down into them. This so upset Giles that he foolishly gave him two quarts of water; Formby simply swallowed this and fell down and died, his eyes so sunken that they were almost hidden in his head. Giles was not unwilling to follow him.

Jimmy now brought the camels into camp, and 'they looked knowingly at the prostrate form of the dead horse', and knelt to receive the horse's load. These calm patient creatures were now the only hope of the three men. There was only three pints of water left for men and beasts. Giles, the least gloomy of men, was so weak and near delirium that he began to admit despair, and at night through the locking branches of the scrub saw death between the stars. Sleeplessly thinking about space and eternity, he was just going to sleep, when he was stirred up and on by the dawn.

It was now the eighth day of continued travel since Wynbring, and Finniss Springs was at least 100 miles away. Old Jimmy was nearly dead, and Nicholls was delirious, throwing his hat in the air and shouting 'Water' where none existed. Only the camels would have lived another day had Giles not seen a whitish light through the mulga and come upon an enormous dry clay pan at four o'clock in the afternoon, and found at the end of it a channel full of yellow water.

'I could not resist the temptation to drink before I went after them. By the time I had drank they had gone on several hundred yards; when I called to them and flung up my hat, they were so stupid with thirst, and disappointment, that they never moved towards me, but stood staring until I took the camels' nose-rope in my hand, and, pointing to my knees, which were covered with yellow mud, simply said "water"; then, when I led the camels to the place, down these poor fellows went on their knees, in the mud and water, and drank, and drank, and I again knelt down and drank, and drank. Oh, dear reader, if you have never suffered thirst you can form no conception what agony it is. But talk about drinking, I couldn't have believed that even thirsty camels could have swallowed such enormous quantities of fluid.

'It was delightful to watch the poor creatures visibly swelling before our eyes. I am sure the big bull Mustara must have taken down fifty gallons of water, for even after the first drink, when we took their saddles off at the camp, they all three went back to the water and kept drinking for nearly an hour.'

They were now about 15 miles from the tip of salt Lake Torrens, and 220 miles from Wynbring. The camels had carried them, and the water for the horses, and finally the gear of the dead horses, across appalling country through ceaseless heat, and never faltered. No wonder Giles called them noble animals, and said he could not sufficiently admire and praise their wonderful powers.

Now it was easy going with plenty of feed over the last 80 miles to Finniss Springs, and to make it even better, the weather came on cool. Old Jimmy was so devoted to Giles by this time, and so impressed with the compass that he thought had brought them water, that he promised to give Giles his daughter Mary for wife and 'Mary was a very pretty little girl'. Writing of this, Giles is then unable to cope with the situation except in verse: ' "I to wed with Coromantees? Thoughts like these would drive me mad. And yet I hold some (young) barbarians higher than the Christian cad." '

At Finniss Springs they were well entertained by Mr. Coulthard, the manager, whose father had perished exploring to the west of Lake Torrens, where Giles and his party had so nearly died. There also he met young Alec Ross, who had come up to join the expedition. He was the son of yet another explorer, the redoubtable and insufficiently appreciated John Ross, who laid out the route for the Overland Telegraph line, and was the first man after McDouall Stuart to cross the continent through the centre. On this journey, on 17 March 1871, he discovered Alice Springs. In 1874 he explored about 10,000 square miles of harsh country west of Lake Eyre for Sir Thomas Elder, using camels and pack horses. His son Alec was 18 in 1875.

By 6 May the expedition was assembled at Beltana and

ready to leave. Second in command was Giles' old friend Tietkens. After the 1874 expedition Tietkens had decided to become a land surveyor, and had gone to Melbourne to study for the Licensed Surveyors Examination. He had made nothing out of the journey with Giles. In his own words: 'The Government of South Australia gave us NOTHING! Except for a few pounds that Baron von Mueller had collected for us we were but little better off for our wanderings and privations in the cause of discovery.' Tietkens had a hard time studying in Melbourne. He spent all his money, one can be sure not riotously, and finally was reduced to pawning his mother's watch. Only then did he appeal to Giles' brother-in-law, Mr. Gill, who lent him £10. At the moment when the £10 was exhausted, a telegram came from Giles to Gill asking Tietkens' whereabouts, and whether he would join the expedition to Perth. 'Necessity knows no law, I was compelled to accept, so in due course I took my passage by steamer to Adelaide.' He brought with him the usual box of seeds from von Mueller, for planting in the wilderness. Peter Nicholls stayed on as cook, and the other members of the party were Jess Young, a young friend of Elder's and Saleh, an Afghan camel driver. Another Afghan, Coogee Mahomet, also accompanied them for a while, and old Jimmy was going as far as Fowler's Bay, glad to get away from Beltana where the local natives had not made this foreigner welcome.

VII

East to West

Although the expedition was leaving, it was not plunging immediately into the unknown, but going south to Port Augusta. Giles happily said goodbye to Coogee, who had been both stupid and bossy, and welcomed Master Tommy Oldham, a black boy who had travelled with him on his journey from Fowler's Bay to Eucla. Giles describes Tommy as a great acquisition to the party, a very nice little chap and a general favourite. Old Jimmy of course was delighted to have one of his own people to talk to.

The equipment and stores were of excellent quality, and Giles was particularly pleased with the big leather saddle-bags, which would not only keep precious and perishable things safe from wet or damp, but also survive, without tearing, the constant scratching and jagged attacks of mulga and mallee branches, that had kept them sewing up torn bags on earlier trips. Apart from stores and equipment, these greenhide bags held the simplest of baggage for the explorers. Jess Young, for example, took blankets and clothing that weighed only 32 lb., the clothing consisting of 'two flannel shirts, two pairs of socks, two pairs of leather inexpressibles, and two pairs of boots'. All this for six months in the bush! There were twenty-two camels in all, seven for riding, with old Jimmy and young Tommy both on the one camel, and fifteen carrying an average of 550 lb. of baggage each.

On 23 May 1875 Giles and his party left Port Augusta,

with no prospect of seeing another human settlement for at least 1,500 miles (with the exception of a detour to Fowler's Bay). As far as the Western Australian border, the plan was to travel about half way between the Bight and Giles' earlier routes to Lake Amadeus and Gibson's Desert, which would also be about 200–300 miles south of Forrest's route. After the border they would be heading more or less straight for Perth, though no one knew what salt lakes or deserts they might encounter. Actually Giles was plunging into the mirage-rippling distances of the purest distillation of flat, old Australia, where the highest hills are of sand that shifts or rock that has been rubbed down. To the east of the continent there are mountains, and from these come the great slow rivers that cross the vast plains with their double, wriggling line of escort gum trees. Along Giles' route there are no mountains, no rivers, no tall gum trees, nothing but sand or gibber plain, mulga or spinifex.

The spinifex early left its mark on young Jess Young, who was thrown from his camel, as he says in his 'Recent Journal of Exploration . . .' printed in 1878, 'into the middle of an unusually fine specimen, and landing in a sitting position; for days walking was painful, riding out of the question, and after which I had to eat all my meals standing'. However, apart from mishaps, for a while the going was very easy, with water lying about on the surface, ducks to be shot for the pot, the days cool and the nights cold but dewless. Pastoral settlement was already reaching far into wild Australia, and at Coondambo near Lake Gairdner they were able to draw water from an 85-ft well put down by a Mr. Moseley and his men.

Soon they were falling in with Giles' old tracks from Wynbring, left in that desperate rush for water in April. Now there were some pools of rain water in the rocks that had been so bare. The camels licked them up, and then ate with relish the green fringe-like leaves, resembling fennel or asparagus, of a low growing tree (possibly Gyrostemon ramulosus or else a euphorbia). The next morning one of the young bulls was poisoned, and could not move, and then the same thing happened to Giles' best bull, Mustara, that had brought him safely through these sandhills in April. Fortunately within a couple of days, although very weak still, the camels had recovered. On the day the party got moving again, they passed the spot where Giles had left the dying horse's saddle in the sandalwood tree; it was still there.

So were the terrible sandhills, and the dense scrub, and barren Mt. Finke that had radiated heat, now mild in the cool June days that clouded over into drenching rain by the time the party reached the rock pool at Wynbring, where they rested for a couple of days under canvas. Giles (and the young men of the party) was hoping to see pretty Polly and the other Wynbring natives, but there was no sign of any life except an emu which Jess Young shot, and which provided delicious steaks. Saleh just managed to cut the bird's throat before it died; otherwise as a devout Moslem he would have been unable to eat it. There was something very poetic about Wynbring, the lifegiving rock in the midst of the plain in the all-encircling scrub, visited only by wild animals and the wandering Aborigines. For Giles, the existence of the Aborigines was totally distinct from his own; 'But the passions are the same in all phases of the life of the human family, the two great master motives, of love and hunger, being the mainspring of all the actions of mankind.' Giles' humanity was expanding; his attitude towards Australia's savages had been softening ever since old Jimmy, and now young Tommy, had brought him into daily contact with them.

Jimmy, in his own country again, happily led the expedition out to the west-north-west to show Giles some new waterholes, and on 5 June, Giles and Tietkens rode ahead of the others and reached Youldeh, where Giles intended to make a depot for a few weeks. The old slabbed well was filled with sand. Giles was left alone when Tietkens went back to bring the rest of the party along, and as the darkness came down Giles, cold and hungry, curled up under a bush, and like some old prophet in the desert, fell into a dream that was also a vision, for Giles was no dour, pragmatical bushman but a visionary for whom the exploration of unknown earth was a spiritual experience, foreshadowing the promise of exploring heaven. And at times, maybe, the fiery wastes of hell. Giles recorded his 'extraordinary waking dream, when we know we are alive, and yet think we are dead', in his strange mixture of verse and prose. 'Then, while lying asleep, engrossed by these mysterious influences and impressions, I thought I heard celestial sounds upon mine ear; vibrating music's rapturous strain, as though an heavenly choir were near, dispensing melody and pain. As though some angels swept the strings, of harps ethereal o'er me hung, and fann'd me, as with seraph's wings, while thus the voices sweetly sung: "Be bold of heart, be strong of will, for unto thee by God is given, to roam the desert paths of earth, and thence explore the fields of heaven. Be bold of heart, be strong of will, and naught on earth shall lay thee low." When suddenly I awoke, and found that the party with all the camels had arrived, my fire was relit, and the whole place lately so silent was now in a bustle. I got up, and looked about me in astonishment, as I could not at first remember where I was. But I soon discovered that the musical sounds I had heard were the tintinnabulations of my camel-bells, tinkling in the evening air, as they came closer and closer over the sandhills to the place where I lay dreaming, and my senses returned at length to their ordinary groove.'

Safely established at the Youldeh depot, Giles could look back on an easy trip from Port Augusta, over much the same country that had nearly left him to perish in April. So much difference did water make. All explorers of semi-arid Australia had to believe in luck, that they would find a waterhole before it was too late to turn back; a good season, and rain lying in pools on clay pans or in rocks, was like a divine blessing softening the rigours of chance.

While they were at Youldeh the cow camel that Jimmy and Tommy had been riding calved; the calf was not much bigger than a cat. Giles was now obliged to go to Fowler's Bay, to deliver some camels for Elder, and to do some private business of his own. He gave instructions for Tietkens and Young, while he was away, to reconnoitre to the north to see if there was any waterhole where a depot might be established. Jimmy was very excited at the prospect of returning to his wife and children. Again he promised Giles that he should have his daughter Mary, and also that Peter Nicholls should have his other daughter Jinny. But when they reached Colona station, a couple of days from Fowler's Bay, they learned that an epidemic had been raging amongst the natives, and that old Jimmy had lost both his daughters. 'When he heard this, the poor old fellow cried, and looked at me, as much as to say if I had not taken him away he might have saved them. It was but poor consolation to tell him, what he could not understand, that those whom the gods love die young. I suffered another loss, as a bright little black boy called Fry, a great favourite of mine, with splendid eyes and teeth, whom I had intended to bring with me as a companion for Tommy, was also dead. I parted from old Jimmy the best of friends, but he was like Rachel weeping for her children, and would not be comforted. I gave him money and presents, and dresses for his wife, and anything he asked for, but this was not very much.'

Old Jimmy's poignant grief was in marked contrast to Tommy Oldham's reception of the news, on Giles' return to Youldeh, that his father had died in the epidemic. They broke the news to him very gently, and Tommy came up to Giles and said, ' "Oh, Mr. Giles, my"—adjective (not) blooming—"old father is dead too." I said, "Is that how you talk of your poor old father, Tommy, now that he is dead?" To this he replied, much in the same way as some civilized sons may often have done, "Well, I couldn't help it!" '

Giles in his written narrative seems to be amused, even horrified, at old Jimmy's generous offer of his daughter Mary. One wonders what sex life, if any, Giles had. Like many old pioneering bushmen, he never married. Yet many of these same old bushmen fathered half-castes all over Australia on the aboriginal women they pretended in public to despise. Even Giles, with all his uncomplimentary remarks about the ugliness and dirt of the Aborigines, was obviously attracted by pretty Polly at Wynbring who, 'enchantingly bashful', embraced him, naked. There are rumours today of an old half-caste in the Warburton Range who was always known as Giles' son. Although the explorers and the old bushmen, the itinerant pastoral workers, established the closest practical links with Australia naming its features and working its soil, they were strangely impermanent in their human contacts. Like clouds they drifted together with the Aborigines and drifted away again, and the children they had were like seedlings of mulga or desert oak brought swiftly up by rare rain, beautiful and hardy but left to fend for themselves in the red sand.

While Giles was away at Fowler's Bay, Tietkens and Young

and Tommy made a useful examination of the country to the north-west, penetrating into heavy sandhills and endless scrub, but on their return finding a pretty, open, grassy plain, and a good native well, at a place the natives called Ooldabinna, about 92 miles from Youldeh. This was not far from what is now an atomic weapons test site, at Maralinga. Giles was very pleased with this information on his return towards the end of the month, as it gave him a further depot. On 27 July the expedition left Youldeh with 19 camels and provisions for eight months, and 'a perfect equipment for carrying water'. After five and a half days' travelling they reached Ooldabinna, which was as pretty as Tietkens had said, but Giles was disappointed with the water supply. The camels did not drink on arrival, but the next day they did, and emptied all the waterholes, leaving the human members of the party dependent on the soakage, which was very slow. At least the ground was carpeted with an attractive little plant like mignonette, on which the camels happily grazed.

Giles now decided to send Tietkens and Young again to the north, while he would reconnoitre to the west. Part of the reason for Giles' success as a leader was that he was not jealous of his subordinates, and did not want to make every discovery himself. The chances were that much the most interesting country would be to the north, but he went to the west. 'I was desirous, as were they, that my two officers should share the honour of completing a line of discovery from Youldeh, northwards to the Everard and Musgrave Ranges, and thus connect those considerable geographical features with the coast-line at Fowler's Bay; and I promised them if they were fortunate and discovered more water for a depot to the north, that they should finish their line, whether I was successful to the west or not. This, ending at

Giles' Expedition to Western Australia, 1875: Saleh, Alexander Ross, Peter Nicholls; W. H. Tietkens, E. Giles, J. Young; Tommy Oldham

Attack at the Farthest East, from *Australia Twice Traversed*

the Musgrave Ranges, would form in itself a very interesting expedition. Those ranges lay nearly 200 miles to the north. As the Musgrave Range is probably the highest in South Australia and a continuous chain with the Everard Range, seventy or eighty miles this side of it, I had every reason to expect that my officers would be successful in discovering a fresh depot up in a northerly direction.'

Both parties left on 4 August, Tietkens and Young taking only their own riding camels and one baggage camel carrying 30 gallons of water and ten days' provisions. Giles hoped they would find water within 100 miles. He had no such hopes for himself, thinking it not improbable that he would have to travel at least 200 miles, leaving him the problem of getting home again. So he took Saleh, the Afghan camel-man with camels which would leave two casks a hundred miles out and then return, while Giles would push out further with young Alec Ross and two baggage camels.

Westward, he found more sandhills, more scrub, and then lake after lake, all dry, briny and useless. These are some of the hundreds of lakes so misleadingly marked a fresh blue on maps of Australia. They have a beauty of their own, delicate but sinister, to which Giles immediately responded with all his poetic sensibility. 'At this distance, on the shores of a salt lake, there was really a very pretty scene, though in such a frightful desert. A high, red earthy bank fringed with feathery mulga and bushes to the brink, overlooking the milk-white expanse of the lake, and all surrounded by a strip of open ground with the scrubs standing sullenly back. The open ground looked green, but not with fertility, for it was mostly composed of bushes of the dull-green, salty samphire. It was the weird, hideous, and demoniacal beauty of absolute sterility that reigned here.'

In fact this utter sterility provided the only clear view of the opposite extreme of appalling fecundity, for the extraordinary contradiction of these regions of Australia is that despite being waterless, they are covered in living and dead vegetation. The mallee scrub, with its fountain of long limbs shooting from the huge knobbly root, and its dead branches fallen and criss-crossing, is the most characteristic and the worst to break through. The patches of mulga, casuarina and sandalwood present the same problems, although foliage of these trees hangs down elegantly and softly, whereas at eye-level in the mallee there is nothing but bare wood under a roof of leaves.

Giles found the scrub so thick he could seldom see a hundred yards ahead; Alec Ross put it more strongly, maintaining 'you could not see your hand before you'. At least an advantage was that it was easy to make a thick covering of boughs and leaves over the water-casks they were leaving for their return journey. The scrub swarmed with its own vegetable life, but there was no trace or sound of human or animal life. Giles was certainly used by now to the silence of the Australian bush, but somehow here it was more menacing than it had ever been. 'No traces of any human inhabitants were seen, nor were the usually ever-present, tracks of native game, or their canine enemy the wild dingo, distinguishable upon the sands of this previously untrodden wilderness. The silence and the solitude of this mighty waste were appalling to the mind, and I almost regretted that I had sworn to conquer it. The only sound the ear could catch, as hour after hour we slowly glided on, was the passage of our noiseless treading and spongy-footed "ships" as they forced their way through the live and dead timber of the hideous scrubs. Thus we wandered on, farther from our camp, farther from our casks, and farther from everything we wished or required.'

Even though it was midwinter the days were in the mid-

90's in the shade, and if any water were found, it would be sure to be fast evaporating. On the seventh day out they came on burnt spinifex, and native tracks, and discovered an open space by what looked like a salt lake, where the little purple pea-vetch, and mignonette and the splendid Sturt's pea were growing, providing good feed for the camels even if there were no water. However, this was a clay pan, not a salt lake, and not far away Alec discovered a native dam in another clay pan, containing enough yellow water to satisfy the camels, which drank about 150 gallons between the four of them. No wonder the Aborigines were hostile to the explorers; their whole wandering existence depended on these isolated waterholes, and here were these monstrous animals drinking them dry in a day.

This was a pretty oasis, and they had pigeon for dinner of some beautiful bronze-wings that had come in at evening to water. Giles and Alec put long hobbles on the camels, which were enjoying the feed and water, and went peacefully to bed. But when they woke at dawn the camels were gone. Alec went after them, and by midday still had not returned, while Giles sat waiting, growing more and more anxious. 'If he should be unable to track, and should return without them, our case would be almost hopeless. If camels are determined to stampede and can get a good start, there is frequently no overtaking them on foot. They are not like horses, which will return of their own accord to water. Camels know their own powers and their own independence of man, and I believe that a camel, if not in subjection, might live for months without water, provided it could get succulent food. How anxiously I listened as hour after hour I maundered about this spot for the tinkling sound of the camels' bells! Twenty times during that morning I could have sworn I heard the bells, and yet they were miles out of earshot. When Alec and

I and the camels were all here together I thought this a very pretty place, but oh, how hideous did it appear while I was here alone, with the harrowing thought of the camels being lost and Alec returning without them. Death itself in any terrors clad would have been a more welcome sight to me then and there, than Alec Ross without the camels. But Alec Ross was a right smart chance of a young bushman, and I knew that nothing would prevent him from getting the animals so long as their hobbles held. If, however, they succeeded in breaking them, it would be good-bye for ever. As they can go in their hobbles, unless very short, if they have a mind to stampede, as fast as a man can walk in this region, and with a whole night's start with loose legs, pursuit would be hopeless. But surely at last I hear the bells! Yes; but, strange to say, I did not hear them until Alec and the camels actually appeared through the edge of scrub. Alec said they had gone miles, and were still pushing on in single file when he got up to them.'

All was well for the moment, but there were very difficult problems involved in deciding what to do next. Giles was safe at water, albeit a very limited supply. But he had no idea where he might find the next water to the west; as he said to himself, 'God only knows where the waters are in such a region as this.' He did not know whether to reconnoitre again to the west, or return immediately to Ooldabinna and bring the whole party up to this native dam.

Eventually he decided to go on. After 40 miles he stopped on the shore of yet another salt lake in waterless country, the scrub stretching as far as he could see. They were now 195 miles from the depot. By the time they returned to the native dam the water level had fallen alarmingly. Now, instead of following their tracks back to Ooldabinna, Giles steered south-east, so as to find out the extent of the great plain inland from Eucla. First crossed by E. J. Eyre in 1841, this extraordinary phenomenon was named the Nullarbor Plain by Alfred Delisser in his examinations of it in 1865–6, and Giles' friend Tietkens explored it further in 1879–80. It stretches for about 350 miles east–west, and about 150 miles in from the coast, treeless, waterless and so level that the railway that crosses it has the longest straight in the world, 300 miles. Under the saltbush and bluebush is a huge complex of limestone caves, through whose often tiny entrances roar subterranean winds. Koonalda Cave, about 70 miles east of Eucla, has a main chamber 300 feet long by 200 feet wide, and at the bottom of it lies a lake of water 90 feet deep. No one yet knows how many such caverns exist under the Nullarbor; only owls and wombats explore them.

Giles found the plain beautifully grassed in winter, although there was no surface water. The camels strode forward without interruption, no timber to break through, no spinifex to jab at their legs and feet. However, such easy going was not for long, as Giles had to alter course back to east-north-east, and on 23 August they reached Ooldabinna. The camels had come 196 miles without water; there was barely sufficient in all the wells to give them a good drink. But amidst the welcome from the rest of the party to Giles and Alec Ross, rain began to fall. They were safe for a while, and Giles gave thanks. 'I was indeed thankful to Heaven for paying even a part of so longstanding a debt, although it owes me a good many showers yet; but being a patient creditor, I will wait. We were so anxious about the water that we were continually stirring out of the tents to see how the wells looked, and whether any water had yet run into them. A slight trickling at length began to run into the best-catching of our wells, and although the rain did not continue long or fall heavily, yet a sufficiency drained into the receptacle to enable us to fill up all our waterholding vessels the next morning, and give a thorough good drink to all our camels.'

Tietkens' investigations to the north had been fruitless; they had found no water, and had not even got within sight of the Musgrave or Everard Ranges. There was, therefore, no choice but to go on to the west, or else retreat. It did not follow, of course, that because it had rained at Ooldabinna it would have rained at the native dam 160 miles away.

Nevertheless, Giles decided to load the camels with as much water as they could carry, ' and keep pushing on west, and trust to fate, or fortune, or chance, or Providence, or whatever it might be, that would bring us to water beyond'. Never has the creed of the Australian explorer been so succinctly formulated.

Giles felt sorry for his own four camels, that had to set off again so soon after a hard journey, while the others were fat and rested. They all had names, of course. There was Giles' little riding cow, Reechy; his splendid gelding, a beautiful white camel, was called the Pearl Beyond all Price. Another cow bore the name of the Wild Gazelle.

They left on 24 August, the camels carrying enormous loads of water. Giles gives an extremely vivid account of their progress through the scrub. 'Camels have a great advantage over horses in these dense wildernesses, for the former are so tall that their loads are mostly raised into the less resisting upper branches of the low trees of which these scrubs are usually composed, whereas the horses' loads being so much nearer the ground have to be dragged through the stouter and stronger lower limbs of the trees. Again, camels travel in one long single file, and where the leading camel forces his way the others all follow. It is of great importance to have some good leading camels. My arrangement for traversing these scrubs was as follows:—Saleh on his riding gelding, the most lion-hearted creature in the whole mob, although Saleh was always beating or swearing at him in Hindoostanee, led the whole caravan, which was divided into three separate lots; at every sixth there was a break, and one of the party rode ahead of the next six, and so on. The method of leading was, when the scrubs permitted, the steersman would ride; if they were too thick for correct steering, he would walk; then a man riding or leading a riding camel to guide Saleh, who led the baggage mob. Four of us used to steer. I had taught Alec Ross, and we took an hour about, at a time. Immediately behind Saleh came three bull camels loaded with casks of water, each cask holding twenty gallons. These used to crash and smash down and through the branches, so that the passage was much clearer after them. All the rest of the equipment, including water-beds, boxes, &c., was encased in huge leather bags, except one cow's load; this, with the bags of flour on two other camels, was enveloped in green hide. The fortunate rider at the extreme end had a somewhat open groove to ride in. This last place was the privilege of the steersman when his hour of agony was up. After the caravan had forced its way through this forest primeval, there was generally left an open serpentine line about six feet above the ground, through the trees, and when a person was on this line they could see that something unusual must have passed through. On the ground was a narrower line about two feet wide, and sometimes as much as a foot deep, where one animal after another had stepped. In my former journals I mentioned that the spinifex wounded the horses' feet, and disfigured their coronets, it also used to take a good deal of hair off some of the horses' legs; but in the case of the camels, although it did not seem to excoriate them, it took every hair off their legs up to three feet from the ground, and their limbs turned black, and were as bright and shiny as a newly-polished boot. The camels' hair was much finer than that of the horses, but their skin was much thicker, and while the horses' legs were punctured and suppurating, the camels' were all as hard as steel and bright as bayonets.'

The heat now became very oppressive, well over the 90's, but the compensation was that there was undoubtedly rain in the air. On the night of the 29th one of the best cow camels calved, but unfortunately strained herself so that she could not rise. She was in too much pain to eat or drink, so there was nothing to do but kill both her and her calf. This painful business was lightened that evening by a heavy fall of rain, and by the time they reached the native dam on 3 September it was full to overflowing, and they camped in luxury amidst the magenta vetch and the black and scarlet desert-pea, with open green grass running out from the white lake-bed to the dark scrub, and high red sandhills away to the south. They rested for a week in this peaceful, beautiful place.

But Giles was gnawed by the thought of what lay ahead. Endless scrub, and no water. He longed for open plains, even for bare desert sand, anything for some easy going. Examining his maps he worked out that they were just across the boundary of South Australia, so he called the place Boundary Dam. To the west, the *nearest* known landmark was Mount Churchman, *six hundred* miles away! And although Giles knew that various travellers had visited Mount Churchman since A. C. Gregory named it in 1846, he had no certain knowledge that water was there. He decided to make for it, hoping to God to find water along the way. Calling the party together, he told them his decision, and said that it was a matter of life or death, they must push through or die in the scrub; he offered to provide rations and camels for any who wanted to go back. It was a desperate thing to do. 'But I had sworn to go to Perth or die in the attempt, and I inspired the whole of my party with my own enthusiasm. One and all declared that they would live or die with me.'

On 10 September they left, Giles fortifying himself with verse.

> '*Though the scrubs may range around me,*
> *My camel shall bear me on;*
> *Though the desert may surround me,*
> *It hath springs that shall be won.*

Mounting my little fairy camel Reechy, I "whispered to her westward, westward, and with speed she darted onward".'

For five days they broke through dense scrub, and on the sixth day emerged into a grassy plain, with good feed of saltbush on it for the camels, and hard and good travelling country for their feet. There was a solemnity in the silence so pressing that nobody spoke much above a whisper. For four more days the plain continued, utterly waterless, the expedition still caught in the spell of its solemnity. For Giles, it was country that God had forsaken, and he did not see any prospect of prayer bringing Him back. Allah was much closer to Saleh the Afghan, who had never seen anything like this plain which to him stretched on into the certainty of death. 'It was totally uninhabited by either man or animal, not a track of a single marsupial, emu, or wild dog was to be seen, and we seemed to have penetrated into a region utterly unknown to man, and as utterly forsaken by God. We had now come 190 miles from water, and our prospects of obtaining any appeared more and more hopeless. Vainly indeed it seemed that I might say—with the mariner on the ocean—"Full many a green spot needs must be in this wide waste of misery, Or the traveller worn and wan never thus could voyage on." But where was the oasis for us? Where the bright region of rest? And now, when days had many of them passed away, and no places had been met where water was, the party presented a sad and solemn procession, as though each and all of us was stalking slowly onward to his tomb. Some murmurs of regret reached my ears; but I was prepared for more than that. Whenever we camped, Saleh would stand before me, gaze fixedly into my face and generally say: "Mister Gile, when you get water?" I pretended to laugh at the idea, and say: "Water? pooh! there's no water in this country, Saleh. I didn't come here to find water, I came here to die, and you said you'd come and die too." Then he would ponder awhile, and say: "I think some camel he die to-morrow, Mr. Gile." I would say: "No, Saleh, they can't possibly live till to-morrow, I think they will all die to-night." Then he: "Oh, Mr. Gile, I think we all die soon now." Then I: "Oh yes, Saleh, we'll all be dead in a day or two." When he found he couldn't get any satisfaction out of me he would begin to pray, and ask me which was the east. I would point south: down he would go on his knees, and abase himself in the sand, keeping his head in it for some time. Afterwards he would have a smoke, and I would ask: "What's the matter, Saleh? what have you been doing?" "Ah, Mr. Gile," was his answer, "I been pray to my God to give you a rock-hole to-morrow." I said, "Why Saleh, if the rock-hole isn't there already there won't be time for your God to make it; besides, if you can get what you want by praying for it, let me have a fresh-water lake, or a running river, that will take us right away to Perth. What's the use of a paltry rock-hole?" Then he said solemnly "Ah, Mr. Gile, you not religious." '

On the eleventh day they came into some scrub again, and at sundown on the twelfth day they came into a little hollow, where there was a large clay-pan, and signs of the presence of natives. But there was not a drop of water, nor signs of it having been there. 'The grass was white and dry, and ready to blow away with any wind.'

They were now 242 miles from the last water, and Giles gave the camels a day's rest, listening to 'the croaking of ravens of some of the party', who were urging Giles to shoot some of the camels so as to save water for the others and the human members of the party. Giles refused; in a rather misplaced metaphor, he said they would all sink, or all swim. He shared out 80 gallons between the eighteen grown camels and the calf; not much more than four gallons each, or the equivalent of four thimblefuls to a man. 'To give away this quantity of water in such a region was like parting with our blood; but it was the creatures' right, and carried expressly for them; and with the renewed vigour which even that small quantity imparted to them, our own lives seemed to obtain a new lease. Unfortunately, the old cow which calved at Youldeh, and whose she-calf is the prettiest and nicest little pet in the world, has begun to fail in her milk, and I am afraid the young animal will be unable to hold out to the end of this desert, if indeed it has an end this side of Perth.'

Once more heading into scrub, they came out into high, rolling red sandhills, with cypress pine on the hills and spinifex in the depressions. At least for the camels there was a good growth of the broad-leaved native poplar, and they took great bites at these as they went along. The only extra food for the human members of the party was a few mallee-fowl eggs and a scrub turkey Young had shot on the plain. The days continued between 95° and 100°, though the nights were cold.

By now the only cheerful member of the party was Tommy, the black boy. In Alec Ross's words, 'He could never realize that there was a chance of perishing.' Apparently Giles used to carry a small leather bag containing cheap necklaces, pocket knives and fancy coloured handkerchiefs. Tommy always had his eye on this bag of riches. On the fifteenth day Giles, making one of those jokes that are really designed to lift one's sinking spirits, said to Tommy that if they did not soon find water they would all die. 'If we all die,' said Tommy quickly, 'could I have the bag of trinkets?'

On the sixteenth day from the Boundary Dam, towards evening, Young was in the lead, steering by the compass. Giles felt he was heading too far north, and said so. They had a row over it, and Young handed Giles the compass and told him to steer himself, so Giles led the party more southerly by a long white sandhill, to a hollow where they camped. On the next day, the seventeenth, over 300 miles from water, it was Tietkens' turn to steer. To the south-west there was a big depression, and signs of native and emu tracks going in that direction. Tommy became excited, so Tietkens dismounted and sent him on the steering camel to climb a sandhill and see if there were signs of water in the depression. He told him to fire two shots with the Snider rifle if he found anything. Giles knew nothing of this, as he was at the rear of the procession, and when he found out he was annoyed, as he said the boy would only knock the camel up. They had gone another two and a half miles when Alec Ross and Peter Nicholls heard shots. Giles refused to believe Tommy had found water; he thought it more likely that he had knocked up his camel and was calling for help.

But he called a halt, and half an hour later they could hear Tommy galloping full tilt through the scrub, and he 'between a scream and a howl, yelled out quite loud enough now even for me to hear, "Water! water! plenty water here!

come on! come on! this way! this way! come on, Mr. Giles! mine been find 'em plenty water!" I checked his excitement a moment and asked whether it was a native well he had found, and should we have to work at it with the shovel? Tommy said, "No fear shovel, that fellow water sit down meself (i.e. itself) along a ground, camel he drink 'em meself." Of course we turned the long string after him. Soon after he left us he had ascended the white sandhill whither Mr. Tietkens had sent him, and what sight was presented to his view! A little open oval space of grass land, half a mile away, surrounded entirely by pine-trees, and falling into a small funnel-shaped hollow, looked at from above. He said that before he ascended the sandhill he had seen the tracks of an emu, and on descending he found the bird's track went for the little open circle. He then followed it to the spot, and saw a miniature lake lying in the sand, with plenty of that inestimable fluid which he had not beheld for more than 300 miles. He watered his camel, and then rushed after us, as we were slowly passing on ignorantly by this life-sustaining prize, to death and doom. Had Mr. Young steered rightly the day before—whenever it was his turn during that day I had had to tell him to make farther south—we should have had this treasure right upon our course; and had I not checked his incorrect steering in the evening, we should have passed under the northern face of a long, white sandhill more than two miles north of this water. Neither Tommy nor anybody else would have seen the place on which it lies, as it is completely hidden in the scrubs; as it was, we should have passed within a mile of it if Mr. Tietkens had not sent Tommy to look out, though I had made up my mind not to enter the high sandhills beyond without a search in this hollow, for my experience told me if there was no water in it, none could exist in this terrible region at all, and we must have found the tracks of natives, or wild dogs or emus leading to the water.'

By a miracle they were safe, after coming 325 miles without finding a drop of water. As Giles had said, 'fate, or fortune, or chance, or Providence, or whatever it might be' had led them to water. If they had followed Young's original course they would have missed it altogether. If Tietkens had followed straight ahead, as Giles wished, they would also have missed it. It was entirely thanks to Tietkens that they found the water, for it was he who had sent Tommy off to the sandhills. But they would have missed it completely if their general course had been a few miles to the north or south.

The place was as beautiful as Tommy claimed. There was permanent water in the centre of a grassy flat surrounded by cypress pine, and many native wells around, all full of water. The certainty of water was unbelievably soothing. For Giles the dreadful uncertainty had been the worst, more dreadful than any actual physical suffering. He simply could not know whether he was leading six other human beings into an endless waste where they would all die. 'The hollow eyes and gaunt, appealing glances that there were always fixed on me were terrible to bear.' And then, their trusted leader, he had nearly taken them past the water that was to save them.

There have been suggestions that a feud developed between Giles and Jess Young over their argument about the compass course. But Young, talking some years later to the American Geographical Society, had nothing but praise for Giles and his audacity. 'To the enterprise shown by Mr. Giles, in thus risking the fate of the party upon the chance of finding water, may be attributed the success of the expedition. Had we proceeded in the same way as other explorers, we should never have got 200 miles from home. Had we never left one camp until we found water to justify moving to another, we should probably have stopped at the first depot and returned home from there.'

Giles named the water Queen Victoria's Spring, and the desert in which he found it the Great Victoria Desert. They rested for a week in the shade of the cypress pines, while the camels, after alarmingly rushing the water, drank as only thirsty camels can, and the men swam in the waterholes. There were a few bronze-wing pigeons about, hawks, crows, corellas and a collection of strange flying and creeping insects, and some large scorpions and a snake. There were many wild flowers, including 'the marvellous red, white, blue and yellow wax-like flower of a hideous little gnarled and stunted mallee-tree'. There were a number of native weapons lying around, some of them sword-shaped, some boomerangs, and they could see the smoke of native fires far away on the horizon. Three years later, in the United States, Jess Young remembered how awe-inspiring were the nights 'that settle upon those mighty solitudes', no twilight gloaming in the dry air, no sound of human or animal life, and the brilliant horde of stars over the sand still hot from the day.

On 6 October they left their refuge at Queen Victoria's Spring, with the next water, and even this not certain, at Mt. Churchman, more than 300 miles away. Tietkens and Ross had been sent out to leave a supply of water for the camels a day's march to the west-north-west, and now the whole party camped the night at the water, the canvas troughs untouched. A hopeful sign on the next day was that in the scrub there were now beginning occasional fine trees such as currajongs and a handsome eucalyptus with yellow bark. But there was still no sign of water. The biggest excitement was a little hill, the first hill for nearly 800 miles, since

Mt. Finke. But further on, when they reached a granite range about 300 ft. high and climbed it, there was only the discouraging view of endless scrubby rises ahead. An added hazard was a number of salt lakes in their path, in one of which the camels got bogged and the men had to unload them and carry the water and stores, at more than 200 lb. a time, floundering through the briny mud.

A week and more than 200 miles from Queen Victoria's Spring Tommy and Giles found water. The first water was only a small native well, and Giles' riding camel Reechy, or Screechy as he usually called her, drank the lot out of Tommy's hat, refilled by one of Tommy's boots. Tommy then was off like a rocket on Reechy to bring the remainder of the party into the area, but he had gone only 200 yards when down went Reechy on her knees and Tommy cried out 'Plenty water here!' It was a large well with permanent water. As Giles waited by the well for the rest of the party to come in, two native women came in for water, with water-containers or coolamins, cleverly made from strips of the yellow tree bark tied with bark string at the end. When they saw Giles they ran away, then stopped, and looked. Giles 'of course, gave a gentle bow, as to something quite uncommon; a man may bend his lowest in the desert to a woman'. Unaccustomed to such politeness, they cleared off. They were the first natives Giles had seen on this expedition. Shortly after this, the rest of the party arrived, soon followed by a group of native men and a boy, all quiet and inoffensive, and some even speaking one or two English words. Giles found it altogether a romantic and pretty place, reminiscent of Wynbring, and set up camp under some fine acacia trees by a huge, bare, round rock.

Jess Young cut up a red handkerchief into strips for the natives to tie around their heads, and Giles gave them a little

Spinifex, Everard Ranges

Water-holes in Everard Ranges where Giles was ambushed

damper and sugar. All was peaceful, and Young found out on a visit to the native camp that the place was called Ularring. At the camp the men were sitting around with nothing to eat, 'the women being probably out on a hunting excursion, whilst they, as lords of creation, waited quietly at their club till dinner should be announced'. Every morning several of the Aborigines would arrive at the expedition's camp and stay the day; a couple of them announced that they would like to accompany the party on its journey to the west. The favourite visitor was a pretty little ten-year-old girl, excessively thin like all her tribe, but with splendid eyes and beautiful teeth, merry and interested in everything.

'While here we have enjoyed delightful weather; gentle breezes and shady tree(s), quiet and inoffensive aboriginals, with pretty children in the midst of a peaceful and happy camp, situated in charming scenery amidst fantastic rocks, with beautiful herbage and pure water for our almighty beasts. What a delightful oasis in the desert to the weary traveller! The elder aboriginals though the words of their mouths were smoother than butter, yet war was in their hearts. They appeared to enjoy our company very well. "Each in his place allotted, had silent sat or squatted, while round their children trotted, in pretty youthful play. One can't but smile who traces the lines on their dark faces, to the pretty prattling graces of these small heathens gay." '

But on the evening of 16 October, just as supper was being spread, Young chanced to see two natives on the big rock signalling to the two quiet ones in the camp. Instantly behind them a great number of natives came over the rock, all painted and feathered and armed with spears, clubs and other weapons, formed up in well-drilled ranks. There was just time for Giles and his men to get their firearms; he considered that had they been seated at their supper they would all have been speared. There were over a hundred of them, in a solid phalanx of five or six rows, shouting and yelling. Giles 'immediately gave the command to fire, to have the first discharge at them. . . . One of the quiet and inoffensive spies in the camp, as soon as he saw me jump up and prepare for action, ran and jumped on me, put his arms round my neck to prevent my firing, and though we could not get a word of English out of him previously, when he did this, he called out, clinging on to me, with his hand on my throat, "Don't, don't!" I don't know if I swore, but I suppose I must, as I was turned away from the thick array with most extreme disgust. I couldn't disengage myself; I couldn't attend to the main army, for I had to turn my attention entirely to this infernal encumbrance; all I could do was to yell out "Fire! fire for your lives." I intended to give the spy a taste of my rifle first, but in consequence of his being in such close quarters to me, and my holding my rifle with one hand, while I endeavoured to free myself with the other, I could not point the muzzle at my assailant, and my only way of clearing myself from his hold was by battering his head with the butt end of the weapon with my right hand, while he still clung round my left side. At last I disengaged myself, and he let go suddenly, and slipped instantly behind one of the thick acacia bushes, and got away, just as the army in front was wavering. All this did not occupy many seconds of time, and I believe my final shot decided the battle. The routed army, carrying their wounded, disappeared behind the trees and bushes beyond the bare rock where the battle was fought, and from whence not many minutes before they had so gallantly emerged. This was the best organized and most disciplined aboriginal force I ever saw. They must have thoroughly digested their plan of attack, and sent not only quiet and inoffensive spies into the camp, but a pretty little girl also, to lull any suspicions of their evil intentions we might have entertained. Once during the day the little girl sat down by me and began a most serious discourse in her own language, and as she warmed with her subject she got up, gesticulated and imitated the action of natives throwing spears, pointed towards the natives' camp, stamped her foot on the ground close to me, and was no doubt informing me of the intended onslaught of the tribe. As, however, I did not understand a word she said, I did not catch her meaning either; besides, I was writing, and she nearly covered me with dust, so that I thought her a bit of a juvenile bore.

'After the engagement we picked up a great number of spears and other weapons, where the hostile army had stood. The spears were long, light, and barbed, and I could not help thinking how much more I liked them on my outside than my in. I destroyed all the weapons I could lay hold of, much to the disgust of the remaining spy, who had kept quiet all through the fray. He seems to be some relative of the little girl, for they always go about together; she may probably be his intended wife. During the conflict, this little creature became almost frantic with excitement, and ran off to each man who was about to fire, especially Nicholls, the cook, with whom she seemed quite in love, patting him on the back, clapping her small hands, squeaking out her delight and jumping about like a crow with a shirt on. While the fight was in progress, in the forgetfulness of his excitation, my black boy Tommy began to speak apparently quite fluently in their language to the two spies, keeping up a running conversation with them nearly all the time. It seemed that the celebrated saying of Talleyrand, "Language was only given to man to conceal his thought" was thoroughly understood by my seemingly innocent and youthful

Fowler's Bay native. When I taxed him with his extraordinary conduct, he told me the natives had tried to induce him to go with them to their camp, but his natural timidity had deterred him and saved his life; for they would certainly have killed him if he had gone. After the attack, Tommy said, "I tole you black fellow coming," though we did not recollect that he had done so.'

Alec Ross's account of the incident in the South Australian *Register* does not agree, giving Tommy the credit for warning the party of the coming attack. 'On the third day we were having supper under the shade of a rock at 5 p.m., when Tommy Oldham drew my attention to a blackfellow and a little girl, who had been in the camp all day. They were on the top of a rock, making signs, evidently to other blacks on the western side of the camp. As Tommy put it, "That one no good; I think he tell 'em bush blackfellow come up spearing us mob." I told him to tell Mr. Giles, but he did not take Tommy's warning seriously. Tommy showed great nervousness, and would not settle down to his supper, but kept walking about carrying a pannican of tea in his hand. He walked to the northern end of the rock, when suddenly he dropped his pannican and raced into the camp shouting, "Look out, all about big lot of blackfellow coming, and him carrying mob of spears."

'We just had time to seize our rifles, when on top of the rock more than 100 armed natives appeared. They were in close formation and covered in war paint. Just as they were shipping their spears, our leader called upon us to fire. When they were at short range of 40 yards, we gave them the contents of four Snider rifles, and two double-barrelled guns loaded with buckshot. We were only just in time, for another minute's delay we might have all been killed. I do not think it possible that any of us could have escaped the shower of spears they could have sent in. Mr. Tietkens, Peter Nicholls and myself rushed for the top of the rock to give them a further send-off on the other side. On looking round we saw our leader having a rough and tumble with a blackfellow in the camp, and Saleh, the Afghan, hitting him over the head with the butt of his rifle. After a couple of blows the nigger let go Mr. Giles, and disappeared in the high grass near the camp. Saleh said he was afraid to shoot, in case he hit Mr. Giles, and the black had Mr. Giles so pinned that he could not use his own rifle. We could see several of the attacking army were wounded, but with the assistance of the others they quickly hurried away out of sight. We made a great bonfire of the spears, wommeras and boomerangs that were dropped by them on their retreat. Double watch was kept after this, but we had no more trouble.'

It is easy to criticize Giles in the safety of an unbeleaguered house in so-called civilization, but one cannot help wondering whether the Aborigines really did mean to attack the expedition, or whether it was yet another of those tragic incidents in which trigger-happy whites fired first on the blacks. The two so-called spies, and the little girl, may have been doing no more than begging Giles and the men not to shoot. The Aborigines may only have been intending to stage a ceremonial dance for the expedition. But bullets and buckshot make other arguments.

Certainly one of the 'spies' and the little girl (who surely might have been hostages against attack) returned peacefully to the camp, if ludicrously, because they had swapped the garments given them by Giles and Nicholls, and she was now wearing a man's long coat, trailing two feet on the ground, and he a very short shirt.

The following day was Sunday. 'What a scene our camp would have presented today had these reptiles murdered us!'

Giles remembered a Scottish poem about the Temple of Nature, and reflected on God's purpose, or deliberate neglect, in creating waterless deserts, and cursing the Aborigines with the doom of having to live in such country. 'Truly the curse must have gone forth more fearfully against them, and with a vengeance must it have been proclaimed, by the sweat of their brows must they obtain their bread. No doubt it was with the intention of obtaining ours, thus reaping the harvest of unfurrowed fields, that these natives were induced to make so murderous an attack upon us.'

But the evidence does not seem very convincing that 'these reptiles' would have murdered the white men for their not very appetizing bread.

On 18 October they left Ularring. Giles was confident that they would not have a hard journey to Mt. Churchman, a mere 150 miles away, despite the 'dense and odious scrubs'. These were, indeed, some of the worst they had encountered. The mallee had its consolations, however, in the frequency of the great mallee-hen nests, from which they extracted about thirty eggs a day; 'the older eggs', remarks Young, 'being of course more mature than the fresh-laid ones, were less highly prized by those members of the party whose delicacy of taste was not fully developed.' Young goes on to say that by this time they were all suffering from scurvy and ophthalmia, and on waking in the morning it sometimes took half an hour fully to unseal their eyes. 'Our clothing showed the effects of rough usage; buttons were very scarce, and the man who could patch his clothing with pieces of the original material was regarded as a fop.'

On the 24th they came to the edge of a cliff 200 ft. high, and there, less than 30 miles away, was Mt. Churchman, the small hill they had set off to reach from Boundary Dam, 600 miles away. On the morning of the 27th Giles stood on its summit, and nearby found a native well which supplied all their needs. The party was complete and fit, except for one cow camel which had staked its foot, and had now dropped back so far they had had to leave it.

Some friendly natives came up, partly clothed, and speaking a few words of English. Civilization was near at hand, and on 4 November they came on the bark gunyahs of an out-station of a nearby sheep station. 'The sheep and shepherd were away, and although we were desperately hungry for meat, not having had any for a month, we prepared to wait until the shepherd should come home in the evening. While we were thinking over these matters, a white man came riding up. He apparently did not see us, nor did his horse either, until they were quite close; then his horse suddenly stopped and snorted, and he shouted out, "Holy sailor, what's that?" He was so extraordinarily surprised at the appearance of the caravan that he turned to gallop away. However I walked to, and reassured him, and told him who I was and where I had come from. Of course he was an Irishman, and he said, "Is it South Austhralia yez come from? Shure I came from there meself. Did yez crass any say? I don't know, sure I came by Albany; I never came the way you've come at all. Shure, I wilcome yez, in the name of the whole colony. I saw something about yez in the paper not long ago. Can I do anything for yez? This is not my place, but the shepherd is not far; will I go and find him?" "Faith, you may," I said, "and get him to bring the flock back, so that we can get a sheep for dinner." And away he went, and soon returned with the shepherd, sheep, black assistants and their wives; and we very soon had a capital meal of excellent mutton. While it was in process of cooking the shepherd despatched a black boy to the nearest farm, or settlement, for coffee, butter, sugar, eggs, &c. The messenger returned at night with everything. Exploring had now come to an end; roads led to, and from, all the other settled districts of the colony, and we were in the neighbourhood of civilization once more. This out-station was the farthest attempt at settlement towards the east, in this part of the colony. It was called Tootra, and belonged to the Messrs. Clunes Brothers, who live lower down the country.'

And now they were passed on from station to station, relishing all those simple things that after weeks of deprivation had become luxuries, eggs, butter, jam, spirits. Giles sent off a message with a letter to Thomas Elder's agent at Fremantle, and then at the Spanish Benedictine monastery and home for the natives, New Norcia, they reached their first telegraph station since Fowler's Bay. There were congratulatory telegrams from the Governor and many of the gentlemen of Perth, and from his fellow explorer John Forrest. It was good to be welcomed, but Giles the bushman was alarmed at the prospect of banquets and balls and addresses. Their triumphal progress gathered momentum after New Norcia, bush children galloping in to see the camels, and their parents whipping up buggies and traps to come alongside this strange caravan. The 13th November was a red-letter day, as on Mr. Phillips' station they enjoyed the society of ladies again; here also John Forrest met them. The towns on the way to Perth received them under triumphal arches and gave them 'sumptuous banquets' and balls. Forrest insisted that at these functions they stay in bush rig, tattered proof of what they had been through. There was a chilly moment at Newcastle, when the Chairman of the Council in his allegedly welcoming speech said he didn't know why they had come to Western Australia, as they had plenty of explorers of their own. Giles made a short reply, and Tietkens put a little humour into his, but good spirits were restored by Tommy, who was too bashful to speak, and when urged, said 'I don't know what to say.' Someone near him called out 'Never mind, Tommy, say anything.' So Tommy rose in his seat and simply said 'Anything', and sat down.

On 24 November they rode into Perth, in regular desert-marching order, to be met by all the city dignitaries, the brass band of the Good Templars, and crowds of citizens. The ladies threw garlands of flowers down from balconies, and flags and streamers and scrolls of welcome were stretched across the street, and two companies of Volunteers lined the roads to hold back the crowds from the rather nervous camels. According to the Perth *Inquirer* the Town Hall was 'gaily decorated with bunting, but the only floral display we observed was a pretty bouquet about the size of a cauliflower of modest dimensions which General Bonner wore on his breast'. There were about a thousand people squashed into the Town Hall, and as the expedition came through the doors the band struck up 'See! the conquering hero comes' and Giles and his men were cheered all the way up to the platform where the Mayor made a eulogistic speech and then presented Giles with an address on vellum.

In his reply Giles drew attention to those members of the expedition that were not present in the Town Hall, the camels. 'The country we traversed may be described as a hideous desert, and under Divine Providence, we only succeeded in crossing it with our lives by the aid of the camels attached to the expedition.' Prolonged cheers.

There was now a round of festivities, more banquets and balls, and a dinner and ball at Government House. But the journey was not really complete until they had reached the shores of the Indian Ocean, so Giles assembled the expedition again, and they rode out of Perth and finally across the high, wooden bridge into Fremantle. Giles' camel Reechy was so alarmed by the crowds that she jibbed, and he had to dismount and lead her, and soon he was completely hidden in the crowd, so that Tietkens rode in at the head of the expedition, and was showered with flowers by the ladies.

Although the expedition was not theirs, the Western Australian Government declared that they would meet all Giles' expenses since the station up the country where Forrest had met them. This generosity, and the extraordinary welcome given them everywhere, partly made up for the disappointment that the journey had been over such poor country. Giles did not know that he had crossed, near what was later Kalgoorlie, some of the richest gold-mining country in the world. For him the real achievement was that he had actually reached the Indian Ocean at last, after all those earlier attempts. The expedition had almost taken on a life of its own, thrusting its head forward like a giant snake across the desert, unstoppable.

He wrote 'I travelled during the expedition, in covering the ground, 2,500 miles; but unfortunately found no areas of country suitable for settlement. This was a great disappointment to me, as I had expected far otherwise; but the explorer does not make the country, he must take it as he finds it. His duty is to penetrate it, and although the greatest honour is awarded and the greatest recompense given to the discoverer of the finest regions, yet it must be borne in mind, that the difficulties of traversing those regions cannot be nearly so great, as those encountered by the less fortunate traveller who finds himself surrounded by heartless deserts. The successful penetration of such a region must, nevertheless, have its value, both in a commercial and a geographical sense, as it points out to the future emigrant or settler, those portions of our continent which he should rigorously avoid.

It never could have entered into any one's calculations that I should have to force my way through a region that rolls its scrub enthroned, and fearful distance out, for hundreds of leagues in billowy undulations, like the waves of a timbered sea, and that the expedition would have to bore its way, like moles in the earth, for so long, through these interminable scrubs, with nothing to view, and less to cheer. Our success has traced a long and a dreary road through this unpeopled waste, like that to a lion's abode, from whence no steps are retraced. The caravan for months was slowly but surely plodding on, under those trees with which it has pleased Providence to bedeck this desolate waste. But this expedition, as organized, equipped and intended by Sir Thomas Elder, was a thing of such excellence and precision it moved along apparently by mechanical action; and it seemed to me, as we conquered these frightful deserts by its power, like playing upon some new fine instrument, as we wandered, like rumour, "from the Orient to the Drooping West,"—

From where the Torrens wanders,
Midst corn and vines and flowers,
To where fair Perth still lifts to heaven
Her diadem of towers.'

The doggerel was worthless, but the true poetry of the wilderness had not eluded Giles. The tough old bushman, bashing his way through the terrible mallee, keeping cranky camels and hot-tempered men under control, had never lost his ability to respond to the chords of the universe beyond the staccato notes of practical affairs.

VIII

Back across the Desert

AMID the fountains of champagne in Perth, Giles was already thinking of the desert, of returning to the sand and spinifex where he had lost Gibson nearly two years ago. While 'the wine merchants became nervous lest the supply of what then became known as "Elder wine" should get exhausted', Giles had asked Thomas Elder for permission to return overland to South Australia, and his always generous patron had agreed. Giles' toughness and determination are incredible; it does not seem possible that anyone should want to go back, not only into the endless scrub-slashed miles of sand and rock and flies and ants, but into the desert which had killed Gibson and out of which Giles had crawled alone with a water-cask on his back. Giles had crossed the continent to the Indian Ocean, but there was still a mystery in the heart of Australia; with the passion of a personal vendetta, he was determined to find out how far Gibson's Desert stretched to the west from that Alfred and Marie Range he had been unable to reach in 1874.

So the plan was made to travel north to Champion Bay, or Geraldton, and then strike east for the Rawlinson Range. Tietkens, always worrying about establishing himself in some career more permanent than that of explorer, decided to return to the East and complete his studies as a surveyor. Tietkens was sorry to leave his old leader, and found that Giles was 'much disappointed'. Not so with Young; probably because of arguments along the way, Giles did not ask him to stay on for the next expedition. However, no grudge seems to have been borne on either side, as Young later wrote most generously of Giles' qualities as a leader. The party now consisted of Giles, Alec Ross, newly promoted to second-in-command, Peter Nicholls the cook, Saleh the camel driver, and Tommy Oldham the black boy.

Meanwhile in Perth nobody was enjoying himself more than Saleh and Tommy. Saleh was giving the young ladies of Government House rides on his camels, resplendent himself with a ring on every finger, new white and coloured silk and satin clothes, covered with gilt braid; two silver watches, one in each side-pocket of his tunic; and two jockey-whips, one in each hand. Tommy was also dressed in finery, shouting drinks for all at the hotels and telling the landlord to send the bill to Thomas Elder. It would seem that Australian attitudes towards Aborigines and alcohol were much more liberal in 1875 than fifty years later.

Giles also records that 'Alec Ross expended a good deal of his money in making presents to young ladies; and Peter Nicholls was quite a victim to the fair sex of his class. I managed to escape these terrible dangers, though I can't tell how.'

The journey for the 300-odd miles north to Geraldton was a triumphal procession about as far removed from the rigours of exploration as champagne from a muddy water-hole. Mayors and Municipalities provided dinners, and each station outdid the last in food and drink. One lady presented Giles with a pair of little spotted pups, which, later, Tommy successfully passed off as baby camels to a tall, gaunt sightseer and his wife. ' "What's them things, young man?" Tommy replied, "Oh, that's hee's piccaninnies"—sex having no more existence in a black boy's vocabulary than in a

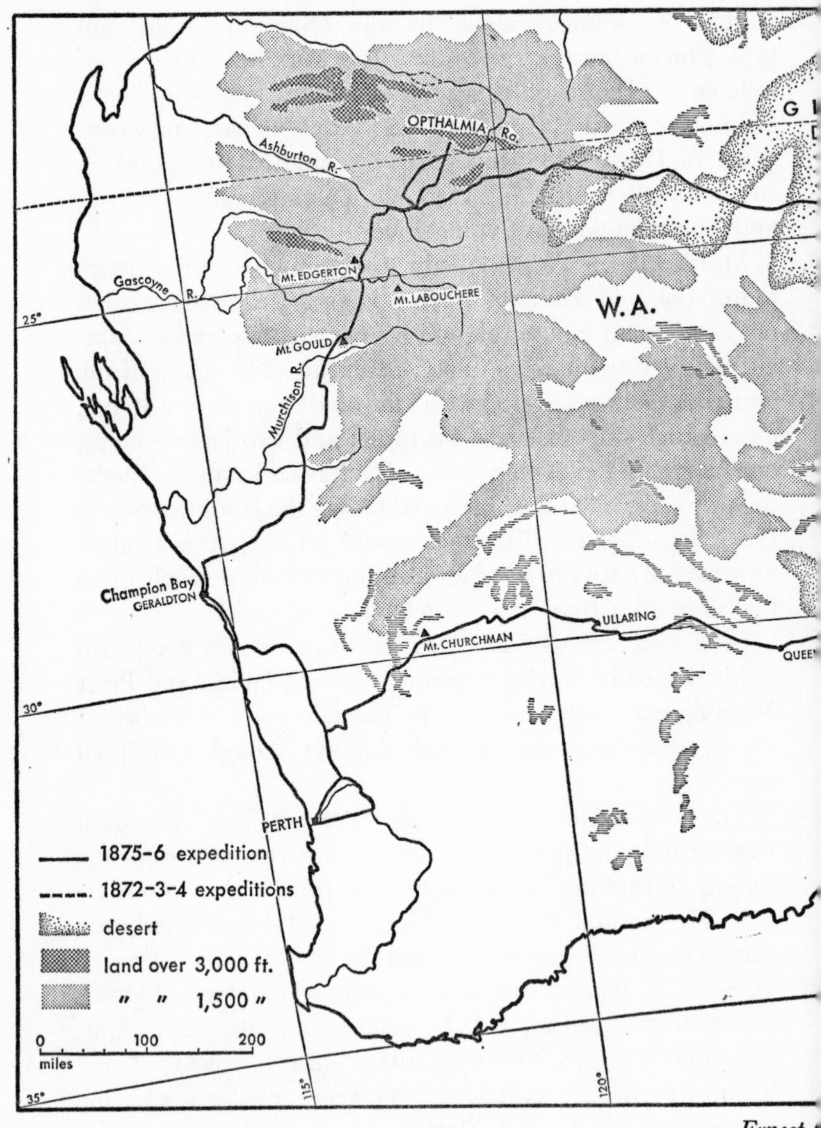
OPTHALMIA Ra.
Ashburton R.
Gascoyne R.
Mt. EDGERTON
Mt. LABOUCHERE
W.A.
Mt. GOULD
Murchison R.
Champion Bay
GERALDTON
ULLARING
Mt. CHURCHMAN
PERTH
25°
30°
35°
115°
120°
1875-6 expedition
1872-3-4 expeditions
desert
land over 3,000 ft.
" " 1,500 "
0
100
200
miles

Ernest

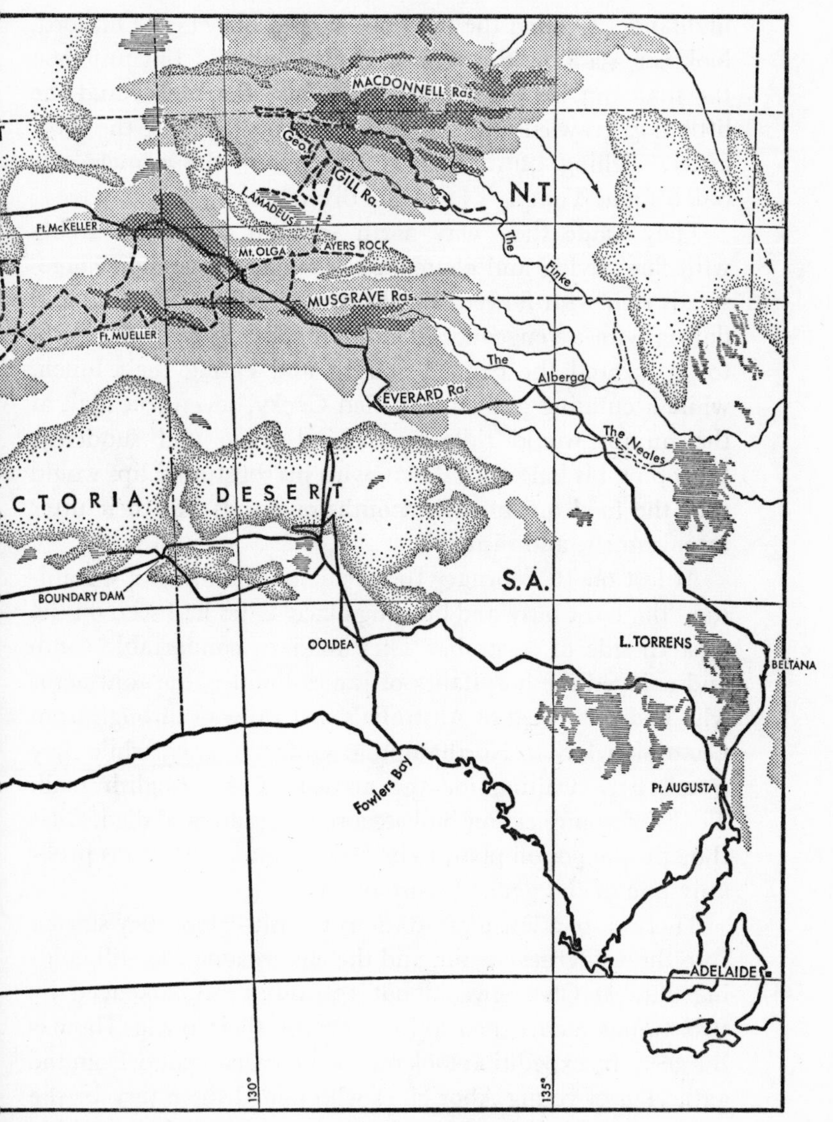

rations from 1872–6

highlander's. Then the tall man said to his wife, "Oh, lord, look yer, see how they carries their young." ' But just then the man put his great head down into the basket and the little dog growled and snapped at his nose, giving the show away. Telling outrageous stories about the camels was Saleh's and Tommy's favourite diversion.

They made their way north through triumphal arches with flags flying and champagne flowing, by station homesteads rich with flowers and fruit, everywhere 'feasting and flaring with a vengeance'. Children came in from the bush, to sit around the camels, staring and eating their lunch, while a cunning old camel called Cocky, seven feet high at the hump, would sidle up behind them and suddenly, 'swooping his long neck down, with his soft tumid lips would take the food out of their mouths or hands—to their utter astonishment and dismay'.

At last on 16 February they reached the town of Geraldton, 'the most busy and bustling place' Giles had seen on the western side of Australia. They made a comfortable camp and enjoyed the hospitality of James Palmer, the contractor who had put Western Australia's first railway through from Champion Bay to Northampton. Unfortunately, while they rested here waiting for the arrival of the English mail, Tietkens' young riding bull ate a poison plant and died. Giles thought the poison plant to be Gyrostemon, but it was probably one of the genus Gastrolobium.

There were a few more stations to visit before they started into the wilderness again, and the champagne was still holding out. At Cheangwa, about 130 miles out, managed by two young men called Wittenoon for their uncle Thomas Burgess, the expedition took on a wild, casual gaiety from the gathering of young Aborigines who joined them just for the pleasure of the walk and their company. There is something extraordinarily touching about the contrast between the expedition of determined white men (not to forget Tommy), prepared with camels and stores and water to risk death in the desert, and the naked, ambling blacks, laughing their way across their home country. 'Some of the girls and young women were exceedingly pretty; the men were not so attractive but the boys were good-looking youngsters. The young ladies were exceedingly talkative; they called the camels emus, or, as they pronounced it, immu. Several of these girls declared their intention of coming with us. There were Annies, and Lizzies, Lauras, and Kittys, and Judys, by the dozen. One interesting young person in undress uniform came up to me and said, "This is Judy, I am Judy; you Melbourne walk? me Melbourne walk too!" I said, "Oh, all right, my dear;" to this she replies, "Then you'll have to gib me dress." I gave her a shirt.'

Their enjoyment of life infected Giles and his party. About eleven miles from Cheangwa there was a big waterhole into which the blacks, men, girls and boys, all tumbled. So Giles went too, and 'we and the natives all indulged promiscuously in the luxury of swimming, diving, and splashing about in all directions. It might be said that—

By yon mossy boulder, see an ebony shoulder,
Dazzling the beholder, rises o'er the blue;
But a moment's thinking, sends the Naiad sinking,
With a modest shrinking, from the gazer's view.'

On Sunday 9 April, having travelled nearly north to Pia Spring, they met Burgess and one of the Wittenoon brothers for the last time. Giles already had champagne cooling in canvas water-buckets, and they had an excellent lunch surrounded by admiring black girls. Did ever another exploring expedition begin quite like this? Disasters might have happened on other journeys, but after such a start it must have been impossible to believe that anything could go wrong on this one.

By Monday all the champagne was finished, and the party left white man's country. But, in Giles' words, 'the harem elected to continue with us'. The country was well grassed and watered, and although the thermometer stood in the high 90's, the heat was not oppressive. The only drawbacks were the flies by day and the mosquitoes by night. There was even wild duck for dinner, and enough to spare for the girls, who seem to have won over all the men except Tommy, of their own race, who although very handsome, was fearfully bashful.

On the 14th an unusual Aborigine joined them; Giles gives a good description of him. 'Here our native escort was increased by the arrival of a young black gentleman, most beautifully dressed in fat and red ochre, with many extraordinary white marks or figures all over his back; we were informed that he was a "cowra man". I had heard this expression before, and it seems it is a custom with the natives of this part of the country, like those of Fowler's and Streaky Bays on the south coast, to subject the youths of the tribe to a mutilating operation. After this they are eligible for marriage, but for a certain time, until the wounds heal, they are compelled to absent themselves from the society of women. They go about the country solitary and wretched, and continually utter a short, sharp "cowra cry" to warn all other men to keep their women away, until the time of their probation is over. Married men occasionally go on "cowra" also, but for what reason, I do not know. The time of our new arrival, it appeared, was just up, and he seemed very glad indeed of it, for he was evidently quite a society young man, and probably belonged to one of the first families.

He talked as though he knew the country in advance for hundreds of miles, and told us he intended to come with us.'

Giles was now making for Mount Hale, on the Murchison River. The country was getting poorer, and he was anxious to get rid of the Cheangwa natives, who were in any case coming to the end of their own territories, although the girls considered they were under the protection of Giles and the other men, and did not care where they went. They cried bitterly at being told to leave, and Giles tried to dry their tears with the promise of presents of flour, tea, sugar, shirts, tobacco, red handkerchiefs and looking-glasses.

The girls were exceedingly amorous, whether married or not, and determined to seduce the shy Tommy. But Tommy was not to be stirred. 'The prettiest of these girls,' writes Giles, 'or at least the one I thought the prettiest, was named Laura; she was a married young lady with one child. They were to depart on the morrow. At about eleven or twelve o'clock that night, Laura came to where my bed was fixed, and asked me to take her to see Tommy, this being her last opportunity. "You little viper," I was going to say, but I jumped up and led her quietly across the camp to where Tommy was fast asleep. I woke him up and said, "Here, Tommy, here's Laura come to say 'good-bye' to you, and she wants to give you a kiss." To this the uncultivated young cub replied, rubbing his eyes, "I don't want to kiss him, let him kiss himself!" What was gender, to a fiend like this? and how was poor Laura to be consoled?'

The cowra man and his friend stayed when all the other natives left, and acted as guides through the harsh, hot country ahead. Soon the expedition fell in with another friendly tribe, whose 'young women were remarkably good-looking, and as plump as partridges; but they were a bit skeery, and evidently almost as wild as wild dogs.'

After crossing the channel and flats of the Murchison River they headed for Mount Gould, and made camp at a channel of the creek at its foot, surrounded by hundreds of natives, some of whom had heard the magic name of Melbourne and asked ' "Which way walk? You Melbourne walk?" ' Apparently the news of the wonderful city of Melbourne had spread for hundreds of miles after one of the Wittenoon brothers had taken a Cheangwa black boy there on a visit.

On Sunday, while the party rested, a swarm of girls and children came into the camp; Giles found them beautiful, with faces 'like the ideal representation of angels'. As usual, he was astonished that such qualities could exist 'amongst so poor a grade of the human race'. And the old women, who were not beautiful, were dignified and quiet, rejoicing in the good looks and pleasures of the young people. The site of the camp was also beautiful, with the rocky ridges of Mt. Gould rising over the tree-shaded creek and the grassy plain dotted with acacia shrubs, but once again the swarming millions of flies spoiled this Eden. Giles was nearly driven mad by them. 'They infest the whole air; they seem to be circumambient; we can't help eating, drinking, and breathing flies; they go down our throats in spite of our teeth, and we wear them all over our bodies; they creep up one's clothes and die, and others go after them to see what they died of. The instant I inhale a fly it acts as an emetic. And if Nature abhors a vacuum, she, or at least my nature, abhors these wretches more, for the moment I swallow one a vacuum is instantly produced. Their bodies are full of poisonous matter, and they have a most disgusting flavour, though they taste sweet. They also cause great pains and discomfort to our eyes, which are always full of them.'

On the 25th they left Mt. Gould and the compass began to work again; the rocks had been almost solid iron, rendering the compass entirely useless. Twenty-seven miles out they found a large pond full of good-sized fish, and Giles named it after the Afghan camel-driver Saleh, 'who was really a first-rate fellow, without a lazy bone in his body', and in particular compliment to the impeccable order in which he kept the saddles, often staying up half the night to keep them in good repair to prevent the camels getting sore backs.

It was as well the camels had a good driver, as the country here was cruelly hard on them, being composed of sharp gullies of up-edged stones which cut their feet while the steepness of the sudden descents often dislodged the saddles and loads. Giles was much relieved to break out of this country into the open valley of the Gascoyne River, 'a delightful and truly Australian scene', where they camped in the shade of elegant gumtrees with upright, creamy white stems surrounded by thick green herbage, with ducks on a long channel of water. 'The trees formed the greatest charm of the scene; they were so beautifully white and straight'.

After resting here for two days they moved on, and on 1 May, the second anniversary of the day Giles had crawled into Fort McKellar after the loss of Gibson, they reached the foot of Mt. Labouchere, a rough steep mass of pink and white granite. Alec Ross and Saleh climbed it, and got nothing for their pains except the sight of endless distance all around, and the certain promise of cut feet for the camels on the jagged rocks of innumerable gullies. A couple of days later Giles climbed a hill and saw 'the most extraordinary, bald and abrupt hills, mounts and ranges being thrown up in all directions; they resemble the billows of a tempestuous ocean suddenly solidified into stone.' It was country worse than desert to cross, and empty of permanent water. Even the Aborigines seemed to avoid it, and Giles was profoundly relieved to be crossing it in a cool month (cool by local standards). He cursed it as 'stony, sterile, and hideous, and totally unsuited for the occupation or habitation of white man'.

There had been odd showers of rain, and these were followed on 8 May by a steady downpour. Snug under tents and tarpaulins, the members of the expedition listened happily to the noise of the rain, but the sense of well-being released by rain in dry places was marred by the disturbing fact that all of them were suffering from what Giles calls ophthalmia, or what would now be called trachoma, or sandy blight. It was not new to Giles; he had had more or less virulent attacks for many years.

On 10 May the creek that they were following led into a beautiful and romantic valley with a large rocky reservoir of the first permanent water they had seen for many days, with the delicious sound of running water echoing softly from the red and white cliffs of rifted granite. Giles called this delectable place Glen Ross, after young Alec.

Leading out from this glen there was a creek which moved into a very broad sandy channel, which Giles reckoned to be the Ashburton River, supposed to be the longest river in Western Australia. Of course it was dry. They followed it for a few days, and at its junction with three or four other creeks, which Giles called Grand Junction Depot, the party camped for thirteen days, exploring the countryside around.

Exploring was all very well, but Giles' trachoma was growing so severe that he could scarcely see, and he had no lotion to soothe his eyes which were agonizingly painful by day and kept him awake at night. Finally he could not see at all, and Alec had to lead the camels, with Giles' camel tied behind them. Not only could he not see; he could not even open his eyes.

Giles sat helplessly while Alec reported on the country

around them, which from a viewpoint on a hill seemed to be on the edge of the desert, with two remarkable peaks away to the north-west, which Giles called Mount Robinson and The Governor, a somewhat schizophrenic compliment to the Governor of Western Australia, who had helped the expedition in many ways. The range which Alec had climbed Giles christened the Ophthalmia Range, with the added irony that he could not see it.

The young man led the blind explorer on, discovering a spring and a splendid waterfall amidst the endless burning rocks; Giles at least could hear the rushing and splashing of the water. Later the water ran into a channel so deep that the camels were nearly drowned crossing it, which Giles found 'rather disagreeable for a blind man'. The next day they were back at the depot again, and Giles kept the party there for two days hoping for an improvement in his eyes. Unfortunately it was very hot, and the flies were appalling.

It is almost impossible to convey to someone who has never been tormented by flies in the interior of Australia just how countless and intolerable they are. This applies to a normal healthy man; it must be infinitely worse for someone whose eyes are already painfully gummed up with trachoma. Giles gives a vivid picture of the misery he and the rest of the party endured. 'It was impossible to get a moment's peace or rest from the attacks of the flies; the pests kept eating into our eyes, which were already bad enough. This seemed to be the only object for which these wretches were invented and lived, and they also seemed to be quite ready and willing to die, rather than desist a moment from their occupation. Everybody had an attack of the blight, as ophthalmia is called in Australia, which with the flies were enough to set any one deranged. Every little sore or wound on the hands or face was covered by them in swarms; they scorned to use their wings, they preferred walking to flying; one might kill them in millions, yet other, and hungrier millions would still come on, rejoicing in the death of their predecessors, as they now had not only men's eyes and wounds to eat, but could batten upon the bodies of their slaughtered friends also.'

As he continued eastwards Giles became more and more disappointed in the Ashburton River. He had hoped for a strong channel, with occasional waterholes, which he could follow for hundreds of miles. Instead, it was rapidly fragmenting into a maze of creeks and tributaries, with no high range at its head, rising from nowhere. The hills where Giles was camped at the end of May were undoubtedly on the edge of the desert, which 'the explorer can scent from afar'. The next sure water could be in the Rawlinson Range, more than 450 miles away. Giles gave orders for all water-vessels to be filled. The icy nights of the far inland of Australia were closing down on them; on the last night of May the thermometer fell to 18°.

By 2 June they were in 'prize and unrelieved desert', surrounded by spinifex, with the first waves of the dreaded sandhills in view. Everything depended on Giles' ability to steer a straight course, but his eyes were still bad and it caused him 'great pain and confusion' to use the sextant. They were now battling with the parallel ridges of sand characteristic of the Australian deserts, and progress was very slow.

Then a calamity struck the expedition. When the camels were brought in on the morning of 5 June, Giles was told that several were poisoned and one or two were dying. Giles immediately injected them with the clyster pipe and made them sick with hot water, butter and mustard. He did not know whether to turn back to the nearest water 25 miles behind them, or risk going on into the desert. Once again, he fortified himself with poetry. 'As Othello says, once to be in doubt is once to be resolved, and I decided that, as long as they could stagger, the camels should stagger on.' Gradually the animals recovered, despite a second bout four days after the first poisoning, but when Giles finally got the expedition on the move again, on 11 June, the camels were gaunt, hollow-eyed, weak and wretched. It was a poor start for the crossing of some of the worst country in the world, although it is not so bad that the Aborigines cannot live there, with their astonishing powers of survival. Giles saw traces of them, and their signalling smokes, and great burnt areas where they had put the fire through the spinifex to flush out game.

In these ceaseless undulations of red sand, with no vegetation to be seen except spinifex and an occasional blood-wood tree or desert oak, Giles was far from the carefree gaiety of those early miles with his escort of laughing black girls. Tough and experienced as he was, this was country that frightened and depressed him. 'The region is so desolate that it is horrifying even to describe. The eye of God looking down on the solitary caravan, as with its slow, and snake-like motion, it presents the only living object around, must have contemplated its appearance on such a scene with pitying admiration, as it forced its way continually on; onwards without pausing, over this vast sandy region, avoiding death only by motion and distance, until some oasis can be found. Slow as eternity it seems to move, but certain we trust as death; and truly the wanderer in its wilds may snatch a fearful joy at having once beheld the scenes, that human eyes ought never again to see. The nights I pass in these fearful regions are more dreadful than the days, for "night is the time for care, brooding o'er days misspent, when the pale spectre of despair comes to our lonely tent:" and often when I lay me down I fall into a dim and death-like trance, wakeful, yet "dreaming dreams no mortals had ever dared to dream before." '

After ten days of continuous travel without water they saw some scattered gumtrees ahead, and making for them found a 'trifling water-channel', but it was enough to set them digging, and when they had formed a good-sized tank, enough water flowed in to satisfy the thirst of all the camels. They had travelled 230 miles from the last well. One of them, poor old Buzoe, Alec Ross's riding camel, had been very sick, and here she lay down and died. She was one of Thomas Elder's original importations from India, quiet and easy-paced, and Giles mourned her.

In this region of no surface water there were many birds, not only the tiny desert birds but bigger ones such as bronzewing pigeons and then a variety of predators, crows, hawks and eagles, which arrived with further reinforcements every day to feast on the incredible bonus of Buzoe's carcass. There were also small wallabies and other rodents, and Alec and Tommy would amuse themselves by watching for an eagle to swoop on a wallaby; as soon as it had its victim in its claws they would gallop up on their camels and rob the eagle of its prize. Tommy was also quite clever at the traditional aboriginal method of knocking wallabies over with a waddy. They were good eating, and also food for the little pet dogs.

Four days' travelling beyond this little oasis, Giles was at last nearing that Alfred and Marie Range which he had seen but failed to reach on his disastrous journey with Gibson. Now he realized how lucky he had been, only having horses, not to have reached it. 'I could not help believing that the guiding hand of a gracious Providence had upon that occasion prevented me from obtaining my heart's desire to reach them; for had I then done so, I know now, having proved what kind of country lay beyond that, neither I nor any of my former party would ever have returned.'

The hills turned out to be low and uninteresting, with no sign of any permanent water, but at the northern extremity they were fortunate to find rain water still lying in a rocky pan. There was enough to water the camels, and the party rested there on 26 June.

After five days more of hard going over the sandhills, Giles could at last see the familiar features of the Rawlinson Range and Mount Destruction of evil memory. The back of the journey was broken. Giles was safely in his own country again, making for his old depot at Fort McKellar and finding the spring running as strongly as ever, though the old camp was all choked up with bushes and his little bridge washed away.

But he was still haunted by the lost Gibson. Saddling up the camels again, taking only Tommy with him, he went back into the desert in the forlorn hope of finding some trace of Gibson. They searched for three days, but could discover no sign of any tracks. However, west of the Rawlinson Range there were some good rock-holes full of water that would have saved the lives of Gibson and all the horses had he only found them in 1874. No matter how skilful the explorer, chance may still save or destroy him.

Calling at the Circus on the way back to the depot, Giles and Tommy found it brim full of water, and the same eagle inscrutably sitting on the same crag. The poetic parallel instantly occurred to Giles: 'Prometheus-like, apparently chained to the rock'.

It was an easy journey on, past old favourites like Sladen Water and the Pass of the Abencerrages, while all the springs were running and vivid green across the Petermann Range showed that rain had fallen there. Giles decided, when he was nearly at the eastern end of the Musgrave Ranges (he had with difficulty restrained himself from revisiting Mt. Olga), to head for the Telegraph Line by a new track through the Everard Range.

Though lacking the prodigious grandeur of Ayers Rock and Mt. Olga, the giant rocks of the Everard Range are unlike anything else in the world, the red granite humped and scooped into every weird shape around flat beautiful valleys where parrots with blue bonnets and green chests fly between the tall white trees. At nightfall and dawn both the colours and the shapes of the rocks become so dramatic that one has an uneasy sense of being in a theatre where some supernatural force is changing the scenery. A frozen shape of a dingo or emu on the hard line of rock suddenly moves, the trees are dead black against the striped sky, and then the light begins to pour down the funnels of rock across the red floor of sand. No wonder Giles thought them 'the most extraordinary ranges one could possibly imagine, if indeed any one could imagine such a scene'.

There was no water at all to be found amongst the great rocks, until some natives appeared and showed Giles where to dig for water. The poor natives were then scandalized at how much the camels drank; to make up for the loss of their water they stole anything they could from the camp in the way of ration bags, towels, socks and so on. However, the natives showed Giles another place, forming a closed-in arena of rock pools on different levels, much overgrown with the native fig trees. Giles mentally noted that any party camped there would be completely hemmed in; he was quite right, for later on, on another expedition, he and his party nearly lost their lives there. On this visit the natives were particularly amiable, especially (and as always) the young ones and the children; rightly or wrongly Giles hated the 'vile and wicked old men . . . who excite the passions of the juniors of the tribe to commit all sorts of atrocities'.

On 9 August they moved south into good mulga country, and then east towards the Telegraph Line, which they reached at Mt. O'Halloran, about sixty miles from the Peake Telegraph Station. Paradoxically, these last fourteen days were not easy, the country being extremely dry even though its features were all familiar. Giles' old friend Mr. Chandler and everyone else at the place welcomed the expedition when it finally arrived at the Peake on 23 August 1876.

The journey was as good as over. At Beltana the camels were returned to their depot, and then the dinners and the banquets and the toasts in champagne began. However, it may be that Giles celebrated too well at Beltana, for while driving down to Blinman, where another dinner was prepared for him, his buggy ran off the road and capsized. Giles was thrown out and a wheel ran over him, breaking his nose and giving him a severe shaking. It was an absurd accident to happen to someone who had just travelled 5,000 miles on a camel. But the tough old bushman did not miss a party, either at Blinman or Burra or Gawler, all the way down to Adelaide, where they were met with carriages and cheering crowds and taken to the Town Hall to be presented with an address by Caleb Peacock, the Mayor.

The honours were to follow, the inadequate rewards for five cruel and disappointing expeditions across deserts and through the sharp barriers of dense scrub with never enough water. Giles was given the Patron's Gold Medal of the Royal Geographical Society of London, and King Victor Emmanuel of Italy sent him a decoration and diploma of Knighthood, of the Order of the Crown of Italy.

With a very few notable exceptions such as Forrest, Australian explorers were rewarded for their incredible efforts with nothing more than a few medals, some immediate acclaim, and then total neglect. Governments gave them nothing, and, as they had not gone looking for mineral or pastoral riches for themselves, they took nothing from the country.

Giles was no exception. He wrote to the Governments of Victoria, Western Australia and South Australia applying for a grant of land, or even for a rent-free lease of land in some area he had first explored, such as the Musgrave Ranges. He was refused by all, even by South Australia where his application was most warmly supported by that admirable man Thomas Elder.

This is all the more surprising, not to add petty and mean, in that Lord Carnarvon, the Colonial Secretary, wrote from Downing Street to Sir Anthony Musgrave, Governor of South Australia, in June 1876 (i.e. before Giles' return from his last expedition), recommending that the South Australian Government grant Giles some land. Carnarvon pointed out that Giles had applied for grants to the Victorian and Western Australian Governments; Victoria presumably had nothing to offer and Western Australia had just made a generous grant to Forrest. Therefore, Carnarvon concluded, 'it would in my opinion be probably in conformity with the wishes of the South Australian Government and Legislature, having regard to their well-known readiness to recognize and reward merit, to leave to them (i.e. rather than to Western Australia or Victoria) the recognition in some substantial and practical form of the services now rendered by Mr. Giles. I have assumed that they would not wish to be anticipated in so graceful an act by any other Colony and I therefore trust that your Advisors may feel able to recommend that in the case of Mr. Giles the remuneration which appears to me to have been highly deserved should be given by South Australia.'

Alas, there was nothing graceful about the South Australian Government. Musgrave's reply, on 6 September 1876, briefly reports that as Giles was fitted out by Elder it was a private expedition and nothing to do with the South Australian Government. Secondly, under regulations Giles was free to have first priority in taking up the lease of any land he had discovered for a nominal rental of 2/6 per square mile per annum. Thirdly, since so much of his exploration was done in Western Australia, then why should South Australia reward him?

This is a fine example of the official attitude to a man like Giles, to his exploration of thousands of miles of terrible country, with 'courage, judgement, and perseverance in the face of very considerable difficulties, and also at great personal risk', to use Elder's words. Even grimmer testimony, perhaps, is the letter of the South Australian Chief Secretary's Under Secretary, J. Boothby, to Elder on 9 October 1876. 'Sir—I have the honour to acknowledge receipt of your letter of the 4th instant, enclosing a communication (1449/76) from Mr. Ernest Giles on the subject of a grant of land being made to him, in recognition of his services in the cause of exploration. In reply, I am to inform you that the Govt. regret they cannot comply with this request, as they understand there is no instance in this Province of an explorer being so rewarded; and they are not aware of any peculiar circumstances connected with Mr. Giles's exploration which would warrant them in recommending Parliament to specially reward that gentleman for his services as an explorer.'

It would be charitable to assume that the Government did not intend either irony or deception. Although it was only too true that neither Sturt nor Eyre had been so rewarded, Warburton had been voted £1,000 by the South Australian Legislative Assembly, with £500 for division amongst the other members of the expedition, and McDouall Stuart had been awarded £2,000 and a lease-free grant of land. But after all, there were no 'peculiar circumstances connected with Mr. Giles's exploration'. No doubt, to one seated in a leather chair in a Government office in Adelaide, the Indian Ocean was only a camel ride away.

IX

Last Years, Obscurity, Neglect

Like old soldiers who rust away in times of peace, old explorers who have nowhere left to go are both pitiful in themselves and a condemnation of the society that pours champagne on their immediate achievements and cold water on their future hopes. Giles, like Forrest and many other explorers, had extraordinary reserves of energy and powers of leadership and judgement, but, unlike Forrest, he did not have the right personality or indeed the ambition to go into public life. When Giles died in obscurity on the Western Australian goldfields, Forrest was Premier of that State and a Minister in the first Federal Government.

Giles was simply an old bushman, possessed like so many of his kind of a poetic soul, but innocent of the hard capital with which to settle the land he had explored and understood so well. At some time during the 1870's he applied for a lease of 1,910 square miles of country he had discovered near Gill's Range, north-east of Lake Amadeus. Although Musgrave in his letter to the Secretary of State of 6 September 1876 says 'under the regulations . . . discoverers can apply for and obtain a lease . . . for a term of twenty-one years at the nominal rental of 2/6d per square mile . . .', Giles, in a letter of 26 March 1879 to the Chief Secretary of South Australia, says 'the rent as you are aware for the first seven years is sixpence per square mile'. In fact Giles, not the Governor, was correct, but even at sixpence per square mile this amounted to a lot of money for a man like Giles to be paying out, with no prospect of any return until the land could be stocked. To make things worse, Giles had spent so much of his own meagre money on his expeditions that he had none left for buying cattle or sheep, and until the land was stocked, only a claim was established; the taking up of the lease followed on stocking.

Apart from some stations along the Telegraph Line, the only country settled in this area of Central Australia was at Henbury, before 1877, and at Tempe Downs and Glen Helen (Giles-inspired names!) in the 1880's; the mid-1880's was the time when most of the famous stations in the Northern Territory were taken up. By the end of the 1880's the rush for land in the Northern Territory had died down.

In 1877 Giles was in Melbourne, hoping that as he was officially a Victorian citizen the Victorian Government might offer him some reward for his labours. He had the support of eminent people such as the Chief Justice, Sir William Stawell, and the Governor's Private Secretary wrote to the Chief Secretary that 'he wanted a grant of land in Western Australia, and was informed that *our* Colony would, in all probability, desire to reserve to itself the honour of giving him a suitable reward'.

Alas, the Victorian Government was no more generous than the South Australian. The Cabinet washed their hands of Giles and 'declined to recommend Parliament to specially reward Mr. Giles. As the original discoverer of land, Mr. Giles would be entitled to take up land upon lease which it is open for him to do.'

In Melbourne Giles was also trying to get financial backing so that he could stock his claim in the Northern Territory. He was not successful, but at the same time his old friend and supporter Thomas Elder told him that the

South Australian Government intended to send out another expedition to the Territory. Giles immediately wrote to G. W. Goyder, the South Australian Surveyor-General, asking for his support in getting Giles the command of the expedition. He was still, and remained always, the explorer rather than the pastoralist. He told Goyder that even were he to make millions out of his claim in the Territory he would still want to command the expedition.

But his luck was out once again. Goyder replied that it was not an expedition that was being sent out (if at all), but only a surveying party staffed from his department.

A year later, after a change of Ministry in South Australia, Giles wrote again from Melbourne to the Chief Secretary asking for assistance. It is a pathetic letter, in which he points out that 'I have made no profit by my Explorations within South Australia and that I lost thereby several of the best years of my life under great privations and without any corresponding advantage'. He goes on to ask for the 'moderate reward' of a rent-free lease of his 1,910 square miles near Gill's Range for an additional ten years, and a non-penalty clause for not stocking it for the initial seven years.

The Government's reply on 10 April 1878 was that such an arrangement was quite impossible without a special act of Parliament, and that 'it would be much better to pay Mr. Giles a sum of money in acknowledgement of his services as an explorer than to allow him to break the law and by that means put money in his pocket'. Once again, nothing came of it, and the 'sum of money' was never found.

To the end of his life Giles continued to apply to Governments and to individuals such as Elder and von Mueller for the opportunity of leading another exploring expedition, but the only occasion anything seems to have come of the old explorer's longing to be back in the desert was in 1882, when he was leading a party exploring the Everard Range.

Since his visit there in 1876, a party working on a trigonometrical survey had been through the Everards in 1880, and had been attacked by the natives. In December 1882, Giles was approaching the Range from the south-west, with 'a very young friend, named Vernon Edwards, from Adelaide, and two young men named Perkins and Fitz, the latter being cook, and a very good fellow he proved to be, but Perkins was nothing of the sort'. He also had with him a black boy named Billy, and twelve camels. At a good watering-place, which he called Verney's Wells, they met up with a lot of natives, not belonging to the Everard Ranges, and white and black alike had a tremendous corroboree in the moonlight. 'After the ball a grand supper was laid out for our exhausted blackmen and brothers. The material of this feast was hot water, flour, and sugar mixed into a consistent skilly. I had told the cook to make the gruel thick and slab, and then pour it out on sheets of bark. Our guests supplied themselves with spoons, or rather we cut them out of bark for them, and they helped themselves ad lib. A dozen pounds of flour sufficed to feed a whole multitude.'

After this innocent jollification they moved on to Giles' old camp amongst the native fig trees in the scooped rocks of the ranges, where they set to work to bale water for the camels out of the upper rock-holes down to the lower. A large number of natives came around and into the camp, and Giles, not prepared to put up with 'the odours that exude from the persons of elderly black gentlemen', ordered them out of the camp. The younger natives left, but the older ones stayed, grumbling threats, and saying that this was their country and their water; it was a familiar proposition, both tragic and true. Near sundown Giles spread a large tarpaulin on the ground, to lay their blankets and rugs on for the night. 'When I had arranged my bed, several old men standing close by, the master-fiend deliberately threw himself down on my rugs. I am rather particular about my rugs and bedding, and this highly though disagreeably perfumed old reptile, all greasy with rotten fat, lying down on and soiling them, slightly annoyed me; and not pretending to be a personification of sweetness and light, I think I annoyed him a great deal more, for I gave him as good a thrashing with a stick as he ever received, and he went away spitting at us, bubbling over with wrath and profanity, and called all the tribe after him, threatening us with the direst retribution. They all went to the west, howling, yelling, and calling to one another.'

Young Verney Edwards was a keen collector of native weapons, and Giles now pointed out to him that here was his chance, for the natives had cleared off to the west, leaving, a short distance to the east, a big bushy tree stuck full of spears. However, it was just supper time, and Giles suggested Verney go for the spears after supper. Verney would not wait, and disappeared behind the rocks as the others sat down to eat.

A few minutes later Giles and his companions heard shots, and grabbing their rifles they ran to Verney's assistance. A line of natives had formed to attack, but the combined fire of Giles' party drove them off. What had happened was that Verney had reached the tree, and was just selecting his spears, when he found himself surrounded by natives sneaking up on the camp. Under cover of the fig trees they would easily have speared the entire party as they sat eating their supper.

They were as astounded at seeing Verney as he was at seeing them, and when he fired the natives thought he was with the whole party, who indeed arrived very quickly. Giles observed: 'We must have risen a good deal in their estimation as strategists, for they were fairly out-generalled by chance, while they must have thought it was design.'

The natives had gone, but Giles decided to keep watch. It was just as well he did so, for some time after 11 p.m., when he was taking an observation with his sextant, out of the corner of his left eye he saw something faintly quivering. It soon resolved itself into a large group of natives creeping out of the mulga towards the creek. Very slowly taking his hand away from the sextant he took up his rifle and fired into the middle of them, and then fired another shot with Verney's rifle. 'A horrible howling filled the midnight air', and the natives fled.

At dawn amongst the weird round rocks of the ranges they heard 'a direful moaning chant. It was wafted on the hot morning air across the valley, echoed again by the rocks and hills above us, and was the most dreadful sound I think I ever heard; it was no doubt a death-wail. From their camp up in the rocks, the chanters descended to the lower ground, and seemed to be performing a funereal march all round the central mass, as the last tones we heard were from behind the hills, where it first arose.'

This sad episode is the last record that exists of Giles' wanderings in the outback. In 1887 he was interested in a Central Australian expedition, but this was eventually sent out in 1889 under the command of his old friend Tietkens. The object of the expedition was to explore the country around Lake Amadeus, and it was sponsored by the Royal Geographical Society of Australasia. Two years later Tietkens joined the New South Wales Department of Lands as a Surveyor. He retired in 1909, and lived to be nearly ninety, dying at Eastwood, New South Wales, in 1933. He was always a most attractive character, and remained so, a sturdy old man wearing as a watch chain the nose chain of his favourite camel, full of stories of his great days with Giles. Mrs. Dorothy Moore, who knew him at Eastwood, remembers 'a little old man, with a ruddy complexion and a pointed beard, sitting in a chair with carved wooden arms. When asked how he was, bringing his hands down with resounding whacks on the arms of the chair, and exclaiming "Ridiculously well, my dear, ridiculously well!" '

In the early 1890's Giles was still living in Melbourne, and once again, in 1892, he was writing to von Mueller offering his services gratuitously to lead an expedition to examine the Great Western Tropical Desert and to search for traces of Dr. Leichhardt's expedition. They would be out ten months and it would cost £300 for the outfit and £200 for the wages. But nothing was offered to him.

In 1889 the narrative of his explorations, *Australia Twice Traversed*: The Romance of Exploration, was published by Sampson Low in London. Although it is one of the most fascinating, and stylistically the most entertaining of books by Australian explorers, it did not bring him either riches or further fame.

In the mid-1890's he went with his nephew Gordon Gill to try his luck on the Western Australian goldfields. He did not find any nuggets, but instead took a steady job at £3 a week working as a clerk in the office of the Chief Inspector of Mines. In November 1897 he contracted pneumonia, and after a few days of illness he died on 20 November.

He died obscure and neglected, and although there was talk of a state funeral, the Western Australian Government kept up the record of indifference already shown Giles by the Governments of South Australia and Victoria. The newspaper account of the funeral creaks like a hearse, but at least the inhabitants of Coolgardie were proud of the old explorer who had settled and died amongst them. 'The funeral of the late Mr. E. Giles took place this afternoon. The attendance was very large. The cortege started from the residence of deceased's nephew, and proceeded to the Church of England, where a service was conducted; thence it went along Bayley Street to the cemetery. The Police Force, the Fire Brigade, the Mayor and Councillors of the town, the Warden, Govt. officials, private friends, and residents were at the grave. Archdeacon Parkes conducted the Services.'

Giles' courage and bushmanship were not only beyond question but also beyond the range of all except the toughest of travellers. To turn back as he did to look for Gibson, when he had only just escaped with his own life; to cross the western deserts again, after nearly perishing in the Great Victoria Desert: these are only the most obvious examples of his quality. Yet failure is an essential part of his achievement, for his work cannot be considered apart from the terrible nature of the country he explored. The man who, after Giles, knew it best, the indestructible and lucky Forrest, called it 'most miserable and intolerable', and said that despite 'our usual luck' it was 'a marvel that we got through at all'. Giles and his sponsors were hoping to open up new country that could be used for stock and for overland routes between east and west. In these contexts his journeys were useless, which no doubt partly explains the refusal of the State Governments to reward him. Neither he nor the politicians were to know that Mt. Olga and Ayers Rock would draw thousands of tourists every year from all over the world, nor that minerals would be more important for Western Australia than sheep or cattle.

Giles can certainly be criticized for his attitude to, and his troubles with the Aborigines. Yet there were others, anything but hot-headed, who also had difficulties in the same areas. For instance, there is Forrest at Weld Springs writing what he seriously thought would be his last words: 'The natives seem determined to take our lives, and therefore I shall not hesitate to fire on them should they attack us again. I thus decide and write in all humility, considering it a necessity, as the only way of saving our lives.' Often the fault was in the whole pressure of history, not in the individual.

There have been other explorers of surpassing bravery and occasional reprehensible behaviour. But none is quite like Giles in the lyrical exuberance with which he greets the unknown. For him, poetry and life are always close together, not only in favourable weather and places, as a flower grows in soil, but in the harshest environments, as spinifex on sand. For all his bushman's ability to go on and get the job done, he claims the poet's privilege to stop and think about the meaning of it all.

He was worthy of the wonders and terrors he discovered, such as Mt. Olga or Gibson's Desert. He wrote his own epitaph, and it was true enough, at the end of his book: 'though I shall not attempt to rank myself amongst the first or greatest, yet I think I have reason to call myself, the last of the Australian explorers.'

Select Bibliography

WORKS BY GILES

Manuscripts

Letters, Journals, Reports etc. in South Australian Archives; The Mitchell Library, Sydney; The J. S. Battye Library of Western Australian History.

Books

Giles, Ernest, *Geographic Travels in Central Australia*, Melbourne, 1875.
Giles, Ernest, *The Journal of a Forgotten Expedition*, Adelaide, 1880.
Giles, Ernest, *Australia Twice Traversed*, London, 1889.

GENERAL WORKS DEALING WITH GILES

Beadell, Len, *Too Long in the Bush*, Adelaide, 1965.
Duncan, Ross, *The Northern Territory Pastoral Industry, 1863–1910*, Melbourne, 1967.
Finlayson, H. H., *The Red Centre*, Sydney, 1952.
Forrest, John, *Explorations in Australia*, London, 1875.
Rawson, Geoffrey, *Desert Journeys*, London and Sydney, 1948.
Ross, Alec, Reminiscences, South Australian *Register*, 31/7/28–4/9/28.
Threadgill, Bessie, *South Australian Land Exploration, 1856–1880*, Adelaide. 1922.
Tietkens, W. H., *Reminiscences, 1859–87*, MS in South Australian Archives,
Young, Jess, Recent Journey of Exploration Across the Continent of Australia, in *American Geographical Society Bulletin*, Vol. 10, 1878, pp. 116–41.
Warburton, Peter Egerton, *Across Australia*, London, 1875.
Willis, Margaret, *By Their Fruits*: A Life of Ferdinand von Mueller, Sydney, 1949.

Index